Frommer's®

D0324575

Montréal
day BY day™
2nd Edition

by Leslie Brokaw
& Erin Trahan

Wiley Publishing, Inc.

Contents

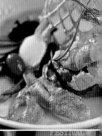

Published by:

Wiley Publishing, Inc.

111 River St.
Hoboken, NJ 07030-5774

ISBN 978-0-470-50734-6

Editor: Ian Skinnari
Production Editor: Jana M. Stefanciosa
Photo Editor: Richard Fox
Cartographer: Andrew Murphy
Production by Wiley Indianapolis Composition Services

For information on our other products and services or to obtain technical support, please contact our Customer Care Department within the U.S. at 877/762-2974, outside the U.S. at 317/572-3993 or fax 317/572-4002.

Wiley also publishes its books in a variety of electronic formats. Some content that appears in print may not be available in electronic formats.

Manufactured in China

5   4   3   2   1

A Note from the Editorial Director

Organizing your time. That's what this guide is all about.

Other guides give you long lists of things to see and do and then expect you to fit the pieces together. The Day by Day guides are different. These guides tell you the best of everything, and then they show you how to see it *in the smartest, most time-efficient way*. Our authors have designed detailed itineraries organized by time, neighborhood, or special interest. And each tour comes with a bulleted map that takes you from stop to stop.

Hoping to soak up the atmosphere of Vieux Montréal, visit the magnificent collections of the Musée des Beaux Arts, or shop in the city's famed Underground City? Planning a walking through Parc Mont-Royal, or a whirlwind tour of the very best Montréal has to offer? Whatever your interest or schedule, the Day by Days give you the smartest routes to follow. Not only do we take you to the top attractions, hotels, and restaurants, but we also help you access those special moments that locals get to experience—those "finds" that turn tourists into travelers.

The Day by Days are also your top choice if you're looking for one complete guide for all your travel needs. The best hotels and restaurants for every budget, the greatest shopping values, the wildest nightlife—it's all here.

Why should you trust our judgment? Because our authors personally visit each place they write about. They're an independent lot who say what they think and would never include places they wouldn't recommend to their best friends. They're also open to suggestions from readers. If you'd like to contact them, please send your comments our way at feedback@frommers.com, and we'll pass them on.

Enjoy your Day by Day guide—the most helpful travel companion you can buy. And have the trip of a lifetime.

Warm regards,

Kelly Regan

Kelly Regan, Editorial Director
Frommer's Travel Guides

About the Authors

Leslie Brokaw has been writing for Frommer's since 2006. She has written or contributed to recent editions of Frommer's Montréal & Québec City, Frommer's Canada, and Frommer's New England. She is based in Boston and is a faculty member at Emerson College.

Erin Trahan is a writer and editor based in Boston.

Acknowledgments

This edition of *Montréal Day by Day* draws from the research and writing of Andre Legaspi, who ably authored the first edition.

Leslie wishes to thank her stepfather, Herbert Bailey Livesey, who authored *Frommer's Montréal & Québec City* for over 10 years and introduced her to the region. Erin wishes to thank the many Quebecois who helped her try to properly pronounce her French-Canadian last name.

An Additional Note

Please be advised that travel information is subject to change at any time—and this is especially true of prices. We therefore suggest that you write or call ahead for confirmation when making your travel plans. The authors, editors, and publisher cannot be held responsible for the experiences of readers while traveling. Your safety is important to us, however, so we encourage you to stay alert and be aware of your surroundings.

Star Ratings, Icons & Abbreviations

Every hotel, restaurant, and attraction listing in this guide has been ranked for quality, value, service, amenities, and special features using a **star-rating system.** Hotels, restaurants, attractions, shopping, and nightlife are rated on a scale of zero stars (recommended) to three stars (exceptional). In addition to the star-rating system, we also use a **kids icon** to point out the best bets for families. Within each tour, we recommend cafes, bars, or restaurants where you can take a break. Each of these stops appears in a shaded box marked with a coffee-cup-shaped bullet ☕.

The following **abbreviations** are used for credit cards:

AE American Express	**DISC** Discover	**V** Visa
DC Diners Club	**MC** MasterCard	

Travel Resources at Frommers.com

Frommer's travel resources don't end with this guide. Frommer's website, **www.frommers.com,** has travel information on more than 4,000 destinations. We update features regularly, giving you access to the most current trip-planning information and the best airfare, lodging, and car-rental bargains. You can also listen to podcasts, connect with other Frommers.com members through our active-reader forums, share your travel photos, read blogs from guidebook editors and fellow travelers, and much more.

A Note on Prices

In the "Take a Break" and "Best Bets" sections of this book, we have used a system of dollar signs to show a range of costs for 1 night in a hotel (the price of a double-occupancy room) or the cost of an entree at a restaurant. Use the following table to decipher the dollar signs:

Cost	Hotels	Restaurants
$	under C$100	under C$10
$$	C$100–C$200	C$10–C$20
$$$	C$200–C$300	C$20–C$30
$$$$	C$300–C$400	C$30–C$40
$$$$$	over C$400	over C$40

How to Contact Us

In researching this book, we discovered many wonderful places—hotels, restaurants, shops, and more. We're sure you'll find others. Please tell us about them, so we can share the information with your fellow travelers in upcoming editions. If you were disappointed with a recommendation, we'd love to know that, too. Please write to:

Frommer's Montréal Day by Day, 2nd Edition
Wiley Publishing, Inc. • 111 River St. • Hoboken, NJ 07030-5774

14 Favorite
Moments

14 Favorite Moments

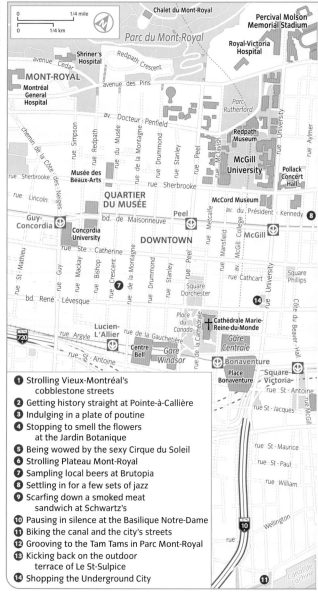

1 Strolling Vieux-Montréal's cobblestone streets
2 Getting history straight at Pointe-à-Callière
3 Indulging in a plate of poutine
4 Stopping to smell the flowers at the Jardin Botanique
5 Being wowed by the sexy Cirque du Soleil
6 Strolling Plateau Mont-Royal
7 Sampling local beers at Brutopia
8 Settling in for a few sets of jazz
9 Scarfing down a smoked meat sandwich at Schwartz's
10 Pausing in silence at the Basilique Notre-Dame
11 Biking the canal and the city's streets
12 Grooving to the Tam Tams in Parc Mont-Royal
13 Kicking back on the outdoor terrace of Le St-Sulpice
14 Shopping the Underground City

Previous page: Old Montréal in the evening.

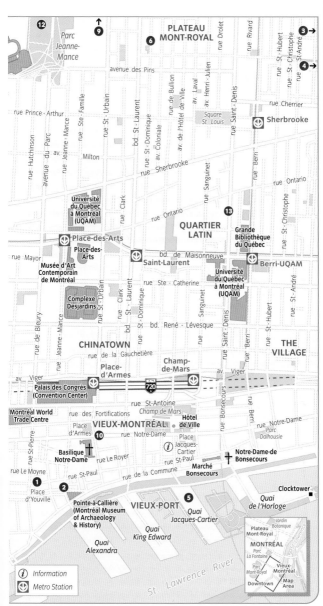

Parc
Jeanne-
Mance

PLATEAU
MONT-ROYAL

avenue des Pins

rue Prince - Arthur

Square
St - Louis

Sherbrooke

Milton

rue Sherbrooke

rue Ontario

Université
du Québec
à Montréal
(UQAM)

rue Ontario

QUARTIER
LATIN

Grande
Bibliothèque
du Québec

Place-des-Arts

Place-des-
Arts

bd. de Maisonneuve

Berri-UQAM

Musée d'Art
Contemporain
de Montréal

Saint-Laurent

rue Ste - Catherine

Université
du Québec
à Montréal
(UQAM)

Complexe
Desjardins

rue Mayor

bd. René - Lévesque

CHINATOWN

THE
VILLAGE

rue de la Gauchetière

Place-
d'Armes

Champ-
de-Mars

av. Viger

av. Viger

Palais des Congrès
(Convention Center)

720

Montréal World
Trade Centre

rue des Fortifications

rue St-Antoine

Champ de Mars

Hôtel
de Ville

rue Notre-Dame

Parc
Dalhousie

Place
d'Armes

VIEUX-MONTRÉAL

rue Notre-Dame

Place
Jacques-
Cartier

Notre-Dame-de-
Bonsecours

Basilique
Notre-Dame

rue Le Royer

rue St-Paul

Marché
Bonsecours

Place
d'Youville

rue St-Paul

rue de la Commune

Clocktower

Pointe-à-Callière
(Montréal Museum
of Archaeology
& History)

VIEUX-PORT

Quai
Jacques-Cartier

Quai
de l'Horloge

Quai
King Edward

Quai
Alexandra

St. Lawrence River

MONTRÉAL

Parc
La Fontaine

Plateau
Mont-Royal

Parc
Mont-Royal

Vieux-
Montréal

Downtown

Map
Area

Jardin
Botanique

ⓘ Information

◈ Metro Station

An enormous joie de vivre pervades Montréal. It's the largest city of the Québec province, the most French region of North America, and Montréal is modern in every regard. It's got skyscrapers in unexpected shapes and colors, a beautifully preserved historic district, and a large area of artists' lofts, boutiques, cafes, and restaurants. Cold and snowy a good 8 months of the year, its calendar is packed with festivals and events that bring out natives and guests in all four seasons. Here are 14 favorite moments in taking in this humming, bilingual metropolis.

❶ Strolling Vieux-Montréal's cobblestone streets and forgetting what year it is. Horse-drawn carriages (calèches) add to the ambience, but it's the old-world feel of the buildings that really transports you back to the 18th century. In summer, you can pop down the rue des Artistes off of Place Jacques-Cartier, the main square, and find prints and paintings of the city for sale. *See p 62.*

❷ Getting history straight at Pointe-à-Callière. In English it's called the Montréal Museum of Archaeology and History, and a first visit to Montréal might best begin here. Built on the very site where the original colony (called Pointe-à-Callière) was established in 1642, this

For a picturesque outdoor experience, you can't do much better than the Jardin Botanique.

modern museum engages in rare, beguiling ways. *See p 27, bullet* ❸.

❸ Indulging in a plate of poutine. Unofficially the comfort food of the Québec province, *poutine* is french fries topped with cheese curds and

Step back in time with a stroll along Vieux-Montréal's cobblestone streets.

gravy. If that sounds off-putting, know that it's better than expected. Packed with flavor (and calories), it comes plain or dressed up with bacon, hot peppers, or even foie gras. La Banquise in the Plateau Mont-Royal neighborhood is open 24 hours a day and has 25 varieties to feed your need. *See p 100.*

④ **Stopping to smell the flowers at the Jardin Botanique.** The city's marvelous botanical garden spreads across 75 hectares (185 acres) and is a fragrant oasis 12 months a year. Spring, naturally, is when things really kick in, but year-round greenhouses are humid quarters to orchids, vanilla plants, rainforest flora, and more. *See p 40, bullet* ①.

⑤ **Being wowed by the sexy Cirque du Soleil.** The world-famous circus troupe has its home base in Montréal and usually sets up temporary tents each spring on the quays (piers) of Vieux-Port, the Old Port district of the city. If you're there when they are, don't pass up the chance to see the magical, mysterious, sensual show. *See p 119.*

⑥ **Spending a whole afternoon and evening strolling Plateau Mont-Royal.** Thick with boutiques, restaurants, and sidewalk cafes, the main drags of boulevard St-Laurent (known to all as "the Main") and rue St-Denis are where to find the city at play and to join in. Especially fun: During 3 days in June known as "Main Madness," boulevard St-Laurent turns into a massive open-air market with designer-dress sales, food kiosks, and ad-hoc outdoor bars where people party into the wee hours. *See p 48.*

⑦ **Sampling local beers at Brutopia and Bílý Kůň.** Montréal is a feast for beer fans, and most bars and restaurants offer at least a few local varieties. Brutopia makes its beers on-site and offers an engaging

The world-famous Cirque du Solei is headquartered in Montréal, and many of its productions have premiered here.

selection each day. Bílý Kůň has local microbrews along with Czech offerings for comparison. *See p 71 and 110.*

⑧ **Settling in for a few sets of jazz.** Jazz may be the most American of art forms, but it is widely embraced by America's neighbor to the north. The monster Festival International de Jazz de Montréal celebrated its 30th year in 2009, and is an annual highlight for 11 days in July. But finding good, live jazz is easy year-round. *See p 112.*

⑨ **Scarfing down a smoked meat sandwich at Schwartz's.** Even with world-renowned gourmet restaurants at their beck and call, returning visitors make it a priority to get to this modest storefront for the Hebrew delicatessen's unique smoked meat. *See p 103.*

⑩ **Pausing in silence at the Basilique Notre-Dame.** Once you see the basilica's ornate and breathtaking altar, you might understand why the church's Protestant architect converted to Catholicism. For a surreal experience, come when the evening light show, called Et la lumière fut (And then there was light), bathes the interior in colors and music. *See p 63, bullet* **3**.

11 Biking the canal and the city's streets. The Lachine Canal was inaugurated in 1824 so that ships could bypass the Lachine Rapids on the way to the Great Lakes. After much renovation, it reopened in 1997 for recreational use. It's now lined with 19th-century industrial buildings and bike paths on both sides. Meanwhile, the city boasts an expanding network of more than 560km (348 miles) of bike paths for commuting and relaxing. *See p 52, bullet* **2**.

12 Grooving to the sounds of hundreds of bongos at Tam Tams in Parc Mont-Royal. Every Sunday in warm weather, Montréalers in the upper Plateau neighborhood wake to this weekly pandemonium of percussion, and never seem to complain. Hundreds roll out of bed and join the musicians or the sunbathers surrounding them. It's a Montréal

Boulevard St-Laurent is a magnet for shoppers and diners.

One of the hundreds of drummers who flock to the park's Tam Tam jam session, held every Sunday in summer.

tradition, so stop by in the afternoon and sprawl out on the grass with everyone else. *See p 54, bullet* **4**.

13 Kicking back on the outdoor terrace of Le St-Sulpice, Montréal's version of a German beer garden. As long as rain clouds steer clear of the city, the large terrace at St-Sulpice is always packed with a young, happy group of Montréalers. Thanks in part to its location on rue St-Denis, St-Sulpice attracts hundreds to its nine bars. One of the best places to unwind on a warm, pleasant night. *See p 111.*

14 Shopping the Underground City. Large shopping complexes built below many of Montréal's busiest buildings are connected by a huge maze of pedestrian tunnels—there's a subterranean town down there. It's a public project where everyone benefits: the city, the vendors, the shoppers. It's an especially appealing option during the bitterest of winter days or the most oppressively humid of summer afternoons. *See p 91.* ●

The Best **in One Day**

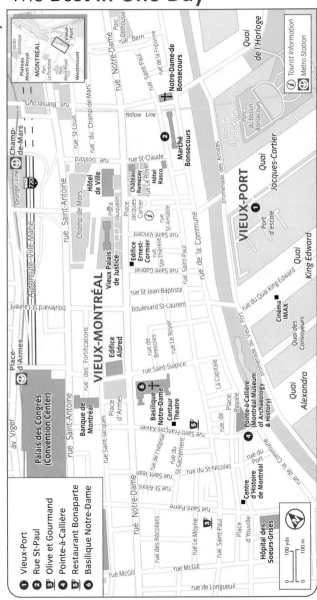

1 Vieux-Port
2 Rue St-Paul
3 Olive et Gourmand
4 Pointe-à-Callière
5 Restaurant Bonaparte
6 Basilique Notre-Dame

Previous page: Stained-glass windows inside the Oratoire St-Joseph.

Center your first day in Montréal around the sites and atmosphere of the oldest and most historic part of the city: Vieux-Montréal. The city was born here in 1642, down by the river at Pointe-à-Callière. Its southern boundary is Vieux-Port (Old Port), a waterfront promenade that provides welcome breathing room for cyclists, in-line skaters, and picnickers, and it extends north to rue St-Antoine, once the "Wall Street" of Montréal. Read up ahead of time at the neighborhood's official website, www.vieux.montreal. qc.ca. START: Take the Métro to the Place d'Armes station and head down rue St-Sulpice to the river.

① ★★★ kids **Vieux-Port.** Montréal's Old Port has been central to its commercial and economic status over the last 200 years, but the port was a dreary area of town until it got a face-lift in the 1990s. Now the converted waterfront and its piers, or quays, are a playground year-round for families, strolling couples, and outdoor athletes. In winter, ice skating rinks are set up here. The popular children's science museum, **Centre des Sciences de Montréal,** is located on Quai King Edward (p 58, bullet **①**). To really immerse yourself, rent a bike from **ÇaRoule/Montréal on Wheels** (27 rue de la Commune est; ☎ 877/ 866-0633 or 514/866-0633; www. caroulemontreal.com) and head out on the path along the adjacent Lachine Canal. There's a summer tram called **La Balade** that scoots back and forth the length of the port, and cruise companies leave from here on daytime trips along the St. Lawrence River. ⏲ *At least 2 hr. Information booth is at the Centre des Sciences de Montréal on Quai King Edward.* ☎ *800/971-7678 or 514/496-7678. www.quaysofthe oldport.com. Tram (May–Sept) C$5 adults, C$3.50 seniors and children 13–17, C$3 children 12 and under. Métro: Champ-de-Mars, Place d'Armes, or Square Victoria.*

② ★★★ **Rue St-Paul.** The main street of Vieux-Montréal (in English, Old Montréal) is full of restaurants,

Locals love to hang out at Vieux-Port on sunny days.

shops, bars, art galleries, and historical venues. Start at the eastern end, near the **Marché Bonsecours** (350 rue St-Paul est). Built in the mid-1800s and first used as the Parliament of United Canada, Bonsecours market is now home to restaurants, art galleries, and boutiques featuring Québécois products. As you travel west on rue St-Paul you'll pass through Place Jacques-Cartier, the neighborhood's main square. At the northern end of the plaza you'll see the green turreted **Hôtel de Ville,** Montréal's City Hall. In recent years, many decent art galleries have sprung up

Montréal's charming and historic rue St-Paul is home to numerous galleries, shops, restaurants, and bars.

alongside the loud souvenir shops on the street. Note that street numbers will get lower as you approach boulevard St-Laurent, which is the north-south thoroughfare that divides Montréal into its east and west halves. Numbers will start to rise again as you move onto rue St-Paul ouest (west). ⏱ *At least 1 hr. Métro: Champ-de-Mars.*

It started out as an earthy bakery painted in reds, pinks, and gold curlicues, but now ③ **Olive et Gourmand** is a full-fledged cafe offering up perfect croissants, scones, and interesting sandwich compositions such as smoked trout with capers, sun-dried tomatoes, spinach, and herbed cream cheese. It's a pity that this eminently appealing spot is not open Sunday, Monday, or evenings. *351 rue St-Paul ouest.* ☎ *514/350-1083. www. oliveetgourmando.com. $.*

④ ★★★ **Pointe-à-Callière.** A first visit to Montréal should include a stop at this Museum of Archaeology and History. Evidence of the area's many inhabitants—from Amerindians to French trappers to

Scottish merchants—was unearthed during archaeological digs here, the site of Montréal's original colony. Artifacts are on view in display cases set among the ancient building foundations and burial grounds below street level. After starting with the 16-minute multimedia show in an auditorium that actually stands above exposed ruins of the earlier city, you can wind your way through the subterranean complex until you find yourself in the former **Customs House,** where there are more exhibits and a well-stocked gift shop. ⏱ *1½ hr. 350 Place Royale.* ☎ *514/872-9150. www.pacmuseum. qc.ca. Admission C$14 adults, C$10 seniors, C$8 students, C$6 children 6–12, free for children 5 and under. Late June to late Aug Mon–Fri 10am–6pm, Sat–Sun 11am–6pm; Sept to mid-June Tues–Fri 10am–5pm, Sat–Sun 11am–5pm. Métro: Place d'Armes.*

At the elegant ⑤ **Restaurant Bonaparte,** adroit service is provided by schooled pros who manage to be knowledgeable without being stuffy. Highlights have included snails and oyster mushrooms in

The Marche Bonsecours dominates the skyline of Vieux-Montréal.

The breathtaking interior of the Basilique Notre-Dame de Montréal.

phyllo dough, Dover sole filet with fresh herbs, and mushroom ravioli seasoned with fresh sage. Look for the table d'hôte specials for the best deal: A fixed-price meal of three courses, for instance, runs C$16 to C$23 at lunch and C$28 to C$42 at dinner. *447 rue St-François-Xavier.* ☎ *514/844-4368. www. bonaparte.com. $$$.*

❻ ★★ **Basilique Notre-Dame de Montréal.** This magnificent structure was designed in 1824 by James O'Donnell, an Irish-American Protestant architect from New York—who was so profoundly moved by the experience of creating this basilica that he converted to Catholicism after its completion. The impact is understandable. Of Montréal's hundreds of churches, Notre Dame's interior is the most stunning, with a wealth of exquisite details, most of them carved from rare woods that have been delicately gilded and painted. The basilica has evening light and sound shows, which are a far cry from the typical Sunday service. ⏱ *30 min. 110 rue Notre-Dame ouest.* ☎ *514/ 842-2925. www.basiliquenddm.org.*

Basilica admission C$7 adults, C$4 children 7–17, free for children 6 and under and for those attending services. Light show C$10 adults, C$9 seniors, C$5 children 17 and under. Mon–Fri 9am–4pm, Sat 9am–3:30pm, Sun 12:30–3:30pm; light shows Tues–Thurs 6:30pm, Fri 6:30 and 8:30pm, Sat 7 and 8:30pm. Métro: Place d'Armes.

The impressive Hôtel de Ville, overlooking Place Jacques-Cartier, is especially picturesque at night.

The Best **in Two Days**

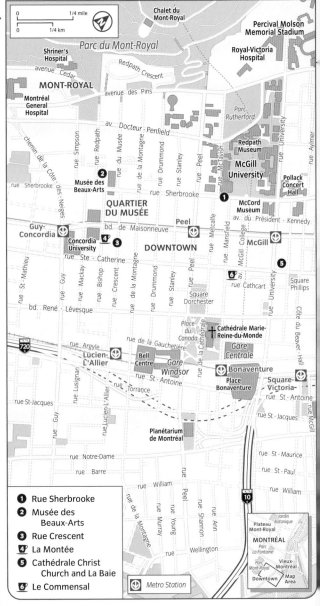

0 | 1/4 mile
0 | 1/4 km

Chalet du Mont-Royal

Percival Molson Memorial Stadium

Parc du Mont-Royal

Shriner's Hospital

Royal-Victoria Hospital

avenue Cedar

MONT-ROYAL

Redpath Crescent

Montréal General Hospital

avenue des Pins

Parc Rutherford

chemin de la Côte-des-Neiges

av. Docteur - Penfield

rue Simpson

rue Redpath

rue du Musée

rue de la Montagne

rue Drummond

rue Stanley

rue Peel

rue McTavish

University

av. Aylmer

Redpath Museum

McGill University

rue Sherbrooke

Musée des Beaux-Arts

rue Sherbrooke

❶

Pollack Concert Hall

QUARTIER DU MUSÉE

McCord Museum

av. du Président - Kennedy

Guy-Concordia

bd. de Maisonneuve

Peel

rue Metcalfe

rue Mansfield

rue McGill College

McGill

Concordia University

❹ ❸

DOWNTOWN

rue Ste - Catherine

rue St-Mathieu

rue Guy

rue Mackay

rue Bishop

rue Crescent

rue de la Montagne

rue Drummond

rue Stanley

rue Peel

❺

❻ av. Cathcart

rue Cathcart

Square Phillips

bd. René - Lévesque

Square Dorchester

Côte du Beaver - Hall

720

rue Argyle

rue de la Gauchetière

Place du Canada

Cathédrale Marie-Reine-du-Monde

Gare Centrale

Lucien-L'Allier

rue Lusignan

rue Guy

rue Lucien-L'Allier

Bell Centre

Gare Windsor

rue St-Antoine

rue de la Cathédrale

Bonaventure

Place Bonaventure

Square-Victoria-

rue St-Antoine

rue St-Jacques

rue Torrance

rue St - Jacques

rue McGill

Planétarium de Montréal

rue St - Maurice

rue Notre-Dame

rue St - Paul

rue Barre

rue William

rue Peel

rue de la Montagne

rue Murray

rue Young

rue Shannon

rue Ann

10

Jardin Botanique

Plateau Mont-Royal

MONTRÉAL

Parc La Fontaine

rue Wellington

Parc Mont-Royal

Vieux-Montréal

Downtown

Map Area

❶ Rue Sherbrooke

❷ Musée des Beaux-Arts

❸ Rue Crescent

❹ La Montée

❺ Cathédrale Christ Church and La Baie

❻ Le Commensal

⊕ Metro Station

A fter soaking in the sights and sounds and tastes of the oldest section of the city on day one, spend day two in the heart of Montréal's business district. Here you'll find the bustle and energy of a city at work, and some of Montréal's grand promenades and cultural offerings. START: **McGill station, and walk north 2 blocks on rue University to rue Sherbrooke.**

Palatial buildings abound along rue Sherbrooke—many were once residences of Montréal's wealthiest citizens.

① ★★ kids Rue Sherbrooke. This broad boulevard is the heart of what's known as Montréal's "Golden Square Mile." This is where the city's most luxurious residences of the 19th and early 20th centuries were, and where the vast majority of the country's wealthiest citizens lived. (For a period of time, 79 families who lived in this neighborhood controlled 80% of Canada's wealth.) Heading west on the street, the main campus of Canada's most prestigious school, **McGill University,** is on your right. Inside the campus is the well-regarded Redpath Museum, the oldest building in Canada (1882) built specifically as a museum. Some of the top downtown hotels are on this street, along with high-end restaurants and shops. Just past rue Stanley, take a peek at the Maison Alcan at no. 1188. It's now an office building that has nicely incorporated one of those 19th-century mansions into its late-20th-century facade. Step inside the lobby to see the results on the right. ⏱ *At least 15 min.*

② ★★★ Musee Beaux Arts. Montréal's grand Museum of Fine Arts, the city's most prominent museum, was Canada's first building designed specifically for the visual arts. It's made up of the original neoclassical pavilion on the north side of Sherbrooke, a striking annex built in 1991 directly across the street, and, set to open in 2011, the adjacent Erskine and American Church, which is being converted into a pavilion of Canadian art. The

Artifact from the Egyptian collection at the Redpath Museum.

permanent collection is extensive, but many come for the temporary exhibitions, which can be dazzling. Past highlights have included the treasures of Catherine the Great, including her spectacular coronation coach, and a show celebrating John Lennon and Yoko Ono's anti-war Bed-In, which was held in 1969 at Montréal's Fairmont The Queen Elizabeth hotel. ⏱ *2 hr. 1339–1380 rue Sherbrooke ouest.* ☎ *514/285-2000. www.mmfa.qc.ca. Free admission to permanent collection. Temporary exhibitions C$15 adults, C$10 seniors, C$7.50 students, free for children 12 and under, C$30 family (1 adult and 3 children 16 and under, or 2 adults and 2 children 16 and under); half-price for adults Wed 5–8:30pm. Tues 11am–5pm, Wed–Fri 11am–9pm, Sat–Sun 10am–5pm. Métro: Guy-Concordia.*

③ ★ Rue Crescent. Downtown's party central. Crescent's most northern block is stocked with boutiques and jewelers, but the next 2 blocks are a gumbo of terraced bars and dance clubs, inexpensive pizza joints, and upscale restaurants. **Newtown** (no. 1476), **Sir Winston Churchill Pub** (no. 1459), **Hard Rock Cafe** (no. 1458), **Hurley's**

Irish Pub (no. 1225), and **Brutopia** (no. 1219) are among the venues that draw hundreds (and often thousands) to the street in the afternoons and evenings. The fun spills over onto nearby streets, with both **Maison du Jazz** (2060 rue Aylmer; ☎ 514/842-8656; www.houseof jazz.ca) and **Upstairs Jazz Bar & Grill** (1254 rue Mackay; ☎ 514/931-6808; www.upstairsjazz.com) presenting great music options. ⏱ *At least 30 min. See chapter 6 for venue details. Métro: Peel.*

Since moving downtown in 2008 from its original tiny venue in Plateau Mont-Royal, **④** **La Montée** has spruced up and become a bit more refined. Curved white leather banquettes and a purple ceiling add pop to the beige and brown decor. Connections are original: bison cannelloni with foie gras cream, blood pudding and mushroom risotto, and beef short rib and tartare with "parsnip different ways," for instance. Pricing is simple: C$15 for one course, C$55 for four courses, and C$65 for seven courses. *1424 rue Bishop.* ☎ *514/289-9921. www. lamontee.ca. $$$$.*

Montréal's Musee Beaux Arts is home to over 30,000 works.

Rue Crescent is heart of Downtown Montréal's nightlife.

5 ★ **Cathédrale Christ Church and La Baie.** This Anglican cathedral, which is reflected in the shiny exterior of the pink-glassed postmodern Tour KPMG office tower nearby, stands in glorious Gothic contrast to the city's downtown skyscrapers. It's sometimes called the "floating cathedral" because of the many tiers of malls and corridors in the underground city beneath it and the way it was elevated on stilts during their construction. It's located on rue Ste-Catherine, the heart of the downtown shopping district. Just next door is the celebrated La Baie, a department store that was incorporated in Canada in 1670 as the Hudson's Bay Company. Its name was shortened to "The Bay" and then, after Québec language laws decreed French the lingua franca, transformed into "La Baie." ⏱ *30 min. Church: 635 rue Ste-Catherine ouest.* ☎ *514/843-6577. www. montrealcathedral.ca. Free admission. La Baie: 585 rue Ste-Catherine ouest.* ☎ *514/281-4422. www.hbc. com. Métro: McGill.*

6 **Le Commensal** presents vegetarian fare buffet style, and you pay by weight—about C\$10 for an ample portion. Dishes include garbanzo curry, tofu with ginger sauce, salads, and so on. Beer and wine are available. Tables have white tablecloths, and a second-floor location at the corner of rue Ste-Catherine lets you watch the world go by. *1204 av. McGill College.* ☎ *514/871-1480. www.commensal.com. \$.*

The Anglican Cathédrale Christ Church, set in the heart of downtown Montréal.

The Best **in Three Days**

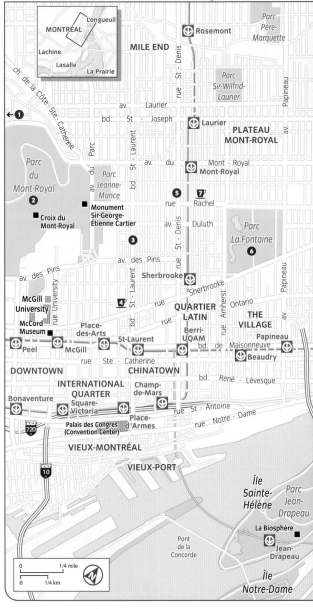

MONTRÉAL
Longueuil
Lachine
Lasalle
La Prairie
St. Lawrence

MILE END

Parc
Père-
Marquette

Rosemont

rue St - Denis

Parc
Sir-Wilfrid-
Laurier

Papineau

av. Laurier
bd. St - Joseph

Laurier

PLATEAU
MONT-ROYAL

av.

ch. de la Côte-Ste-Catherine

1

Parc
du
Mont-Royal

2

Croix du
Mont-Royal

av. du Parc

Parc
Jeanne-
Mance

Monument
Sir-George-
Étienne Cartier

3

av. du

Mont - Royal
Mont-Royal

5   7   rue Rachel

Duluth

rue St - Denis

Parc
La Fontaine

6

Papineau

av. des Pins

av. des Pins

rue St - Laurent

Sherbrooke

Sherbrooke

rue St - Denis

QUARTIER
LATIN

rue Amherst

Ontario

THE
VILLAGE

av.

McGill
University

McCord
Museum

rue University

Place-
des-Arts

4   bd. St - Laurent

rue

rue

Berri-
UQAM

Papineau

Peel   McGill   St-Laurent

rue Ste - Catherine

bd. de Maisonneuve

Beaudry

DOWNTOWN   CHINATOWN

INTERNATIONAL
QUARTER

Champ-
de-Mars

bd. René - Lévesque

Bonaventure

Square-
Victoria

Place-
d'Armes

rue St - Antoine

Palais des Congrès
(Convention Center)

720

rue Notre - Dame

VIEUX-MONTRÉAL

VIEUX-PORT

10

Île
Sainte-
Hélène

Parc
Jean-
Drapeau

La Biosphère

Jean-
Drapeau

Pont
de la
Concorde

Île
Notre-Dame

0   1/4 mile
0   1/4 km

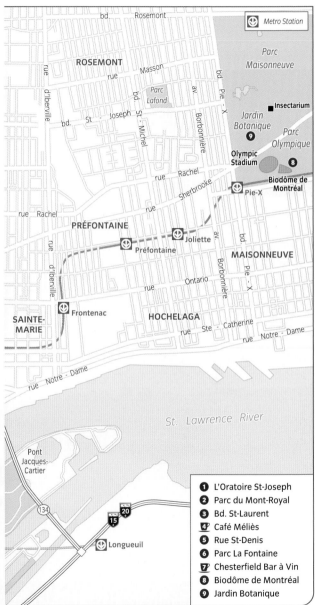

bd. Rosemont

ROSEMONT

Masson

rue

Parc
Lafond

St - Joseph

bd. St - Michel

bd.

rue d'Iberville

Parc
Maisonneuve

bd. Pie - X

av. Borbonnière

Jardin
Botanique ❾

Parc
Olympique

■ Insectarium

Olympic
Stadium ❽

Biodôme de
Montréal

🔵 Metro Station

rue Rachel

Sherbrooke

rue

🔵 Pie-X

PRÉFONTAINE

🔵 Joliette

🔵 Préfontaine

av. Borbonnière

bd. Pie - X

MAISONNEUVE

rue d'Iberville

rue Rachel

Ontario

rue

🔵 Frontenac

SAINTE-
MARIE

HOCHELAGA

rue Ste - Catherine

rue Notre - Dame

rue Notre - Dame

St. Lawrence River

Pont
Jacques-
Cartier

(134)

20
15

🔵 Longueuil

❶ L'Oratoire St-Joseph
❷ Parc du Mont-Royal
❸ Bd. St-Laurent
4⃝ Café Méliès
❺ Rue St-Denis
❻ Parc La Fontaine
7⃝ Chesterfield Bar à Vin
❽ Biodôme de Montréal
❾ Jardin Botanique

The first two recommended days of sightseeing are focused around two relatively compact neighborhoods of the city. For the third day, pick and choose among some of the best parks and strolling areas north of the city's downtown. Like with any great city, people-watching and soaking up its outdoor spirit are as rewarding as visiting its cultural institutions.

Religious pilgrims flock to the L'Oratoire St-Joseph in search of miraculous healing.

① ★ **L'Oratoire St-Joseph.** This enormous copper-domed structure is one of the most recognizable in Montréal, although to see it in person you'll need to trek to the northern side of Mont-Royal (the small mountain just north of downtown, from which the city derives its name). Consecrated as a basilica in 2004, it came into being through the efforts of Brother André, a lay brother in the Holy Cross order who earned a reputation as a healer. By the time he had built a small wooden chapel in 1904 on the mountain, he was said to have performed hundreds of cures. He performed his work until his death in 1937. Many still visit in the hopes of a miracle, sometimes climbing the 99 steps on their knees. Others come to hear the 56-bell carillon, which plays Wednesday through Friday at noon and 3pm and Saturday and Sunday at noon and 2:30pm, all months but February. ⏲ *1 hr. 3800 chemin Queen Mary (north slope of Mont-Royal).* ☎ *514/733-8211. www.saint-joseph.org. Admission and tours are free, but donations*

Picturesque Parc du Mont-Royal draws visitors year-round.

are requested. Open daily 7am–5:30pm (until 9pm May–Oct). Métro: Côte-des-Neiges.

② ★★ **Parc du Mont-Royal.** Renowned landscape architect Frederick Law Olmsted (1822–1903), who designed New York's Central Park, left his mark on Montréal in Parc du Mont-Royal (Royal Mountain Park). The 232m (761-ft.) peak for which the city is named provides Montréalers with a slew of options for recreational activities. Hikers and joggers trek the miles of paths that snake through the park, sunbathers and Frisbee tossers hang out near man-made Beaver Lake in summer, winter sports fans cross-country ski and go tobogganing, and shutterbugs snap panoramic photos from the Chalet du Mont-Royal's terrace at the crest of the hill. **Maison Smith** (1260 chemin Remembrance; ☎ 514/843-8240; www.lemontroyal.com), an information center on the road that runs between the park and the Notre-Dame-des-Neiges Cemetery to the north, has maps for hiking or birding. We offer a suggested walking tour on p 76. 🕐 At least 2 hr. There are several entry points to the park, including at av. des Pins and rue Peel. ☎ 514/843-8240. www.lemontroyal.com. Métro: Peel for the south side, Côte-des-Neiges for the north. Bus: #11 travels down chemin Remembrance.

③ ★★ **Boulevard St-Laurent.** Also known as "the Main," St-Laurent hums with off-beat boutiques and trendy restaurants, packing sidewalks with shoppers, students, and sightseers. Spend some time strolling, snacking, and people-watching your way along the boulevard, starting at rue Sherbrooke and heading north. When the sun goes down, the street becomes a 20-somethings' playground—the

The view from the top of Mont-Royal is one of the best in the city.

dive bars and dance clubs here are immensely popular with the city's college undergrads. St-Laurent is the dividing line of the city: Addresses to its left are all on the west side, and to the right all on the east. 🕐 At least 1½ hr. Bd. St-Laurent, north of rue Sherbrooke to av. du Mont-Royal. Métro: St-Laurent.

The first block of boulevard St-Laurent north of rue Sherbrooke bristles with hipness and money. **④ Café Méliès** is a lower-key cafe-lounge and can be good for a quick dinner, but people also drop in for bountiful breakfasts on the weekends, a midday meal such as arugula lobster salad, or simply an espresso or a glass of wine. Its electric-red decor can best be described as "space-age submarine"—there are portholes throughout. Méliès is open nearly round-the-clock. *3540 bd. St-Laurent.* ☎ *514/847-9218. www.cafemelies.com. $$$.*

5 ★★ **Rue St-Denis.** Parallel to boulevard St-Laurent and 8 short blocks to the east, rue St-Denis also runs the length of the Plateau Mont-Royal district. It is to Montréal what boulevard St-Germain is to Paris, with shopkeepers and people on the street more likely to speak just French here than on other major boulevards in town. It extends from the Quartier Latin straight north, with some of the most interesting blocks between rue Sherbrooke and av. du Mont-Royal. ⏱ *At least 1½ hr. Rue St-Denis, north of rue Sherbrooke to av. du Mont-Royal. Métro: Sherbrooke.*

6 ★ **Parc La Fontaine.** One of the city's oldest and most popular parks, and especially pretty and well used on its northern side. Illustrating the traditional dual identities of the city's populace, half the park is landscaped in the formal French manner, the other in the more casual English style. A small, picturesque lake is used for ice skating in winter, when snowshoe and cross-country trails wind through trees. In summer, these trails are well-used bike paths. ⏱ *1 hr. The park can be entered anywhere on its perimeter. Métro: Mont-Royal.*

There are a ton of great food possibilities in this area—food, after all, is one of the big reasons people gravitate in the Plateau in their free time. **7** **Chesterfield Bar à Vin** is a terrific new option. A wall of wine labels provides some of the decor, and windows open to the street in warm months. In the early evening, patrons tuck around tall tables on stools and try wines, Pinchos (small plates of food), and, occasionally, C\$10 lobsters. *See p 111.*

8 ★★ **kids Biodôme de Montréal.** A terrifically engaging attraction for children of any age, the delightful Biodôme houses replications of four ecosystems: a tropical rainforest, a Laurentian forest, the St. Lawrence marine system, and a polar environment. Visitors walk through each and hear the animals, smell the flora, and, except in the polar region, which is behind glass, feel the changes in temperature. The rainforest area is the most engrossing and includes golden lion tamarin monkeys that swing on branches only an arm's length away (only the bats, fish, penguins, and puffins are behind glass). It's next to

Biodôme and Stade Olympique were both built for the 1976 Summer Olympics and are now two of the top attractions in the city.

The captivating rainforest section of the Biodôme de Montréal.

the Stade Olympique (Olympic Stadium) in the Parc Olympique. ⏱ *2 hr.* 4777 av. Pierre-de-Coubertin. ☎ 514/868-3000. www.biodome.qc.ca. *Admission C$16 adults, C$12 seniors and students, C$8 children 5–17, C$2.50 children 2–4. Discount combination tickets available for Biodôme, Jardin Botanique, Insectarium, and Stade Olympique. Daily 9am–5pm (until 6pm from late June to Aug). Closed most Mon Sept–Dec. Métro: Viau.*

⑨ ★★★ Jardin Botanique.

Montréal's sprawling 75-hectare (185-acre) botanical garden is home to 10 themed exhibition greenhouses. One houses orchids; another has tropical food and spice plants, including coffee, cashews, pineapples, and vanilla; and another features rainforest flora. In a special exhibit each spring, live butterflies flutter among the nectar-bearing plants, occasionally landing on visitors. Its **Chinese Garden** is a joint project of Montréal and Shanghai and incorporates pavilions, inner courtyards, ponds, and plants, while the serene **Japanese Garden** includes a tearoom where ancient ceremonies are performed, a stunning bonsai collection, and a Zen garden. Also on-site is the **Insectarium** (p 60, bullet ⑧), designed

especially for kids. ⏱ *At least 2 hr.* 4101 rue Sherbrooke est. (opposite Olympic Stadium). ☎ 514/872-1400. www.ville.montreal.qc.ca/jardin. *Admission C$16.50 adults, C$12.50 seniors and students, C$8.25 children 5–17, C$2.50 children 2–4. Combination tickets available for Jardin Botanique, Insectarium, Biodôme, and Stade Olympique. Daily 9am–5pm (until 6pm May 15 to mid-Sept, until 9pm mid-Sept to Oct). Closed Mon Nov to mid-May. Métro: Pie-IX.*

Penguins are one of the many species of animals that call the Biodôme home.

City of Festivals

Few cities in North America can rival Montréal when it comes to celebrations. Throughout the year, the city is home to some of the biggest and most heralded festivals in the world, and attending one can make for a very memorable vacation. Among the options to plan around: **Bal en Blanc Party Week,** a 5-day rave that draws an estimated 15,000 people (Apr); **Montréal Bike Fest,** which includes a nocturnal bike ride (Tour la Nuit) and the grueling Tour de l'Île, a 52km (32-mile) race around the island's rim (May); **Mondial de la Bière,** a 5-day beer festival featuring "courses" for earning a "Diploma in Beer Tasting" (June); and the city's signature event, the **Festival International de Jazz,** which for 11 days brings in huge acts and hosts 450 free outdoor performances, many right on downtown's streets and plazas (July). Book a hotel room well in advance if you're planning to visit for Jazz Fest or one of the bigger parties, or you may have to settle for some roadside motel in Vermont. For dates and more information, see "Festivals & Special Events" on p 156.

Travel Tip

In the summertime, a free shuttle bus takes visitors between the Biodôme, the Jardin Botanique and Insectarium, and the Stade Olympique. It's possible to walk from site to site, but the shuttle is handy when it's hot, as it often is in summer. Schedules are available at all of the participating attractions. ●

Montréal's botanical gardens are among the largest and most beautiful in the world.

Historic Montréal

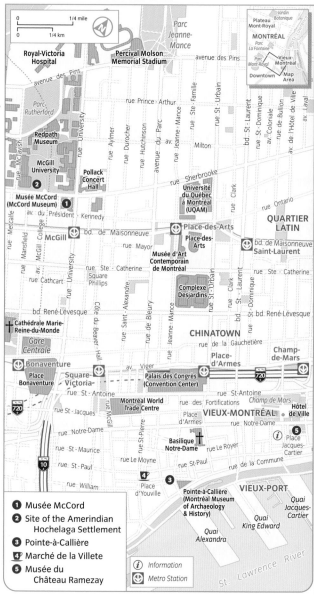

1. Musée McCord
2. Site of the Amerindian Hochelaga Settlement
3. Pointe-à-Callière
4. Marché de la Villete
5. Musée du Château Ramezay

i Information

⬇ Metro Station

Previous page: Sightseeing ships docked at the picturesque Vieux-Port.

First Nations vs. Europeans. French vs. British. Peace vs. war. Montréal history is thick with both strife and tranquillity. The city wears its history proudly on its sleeve: In no other place in North America does the richness of 400 years of nation building continue to be as discussed, dissected, and celebrated as it is in Montréal and its sister city, Québec City, to the north. START: **Métro: McGill.**

1 ★ Musée McCord. The permanent exhibition, Simply Montréal: Glimpses of a Unique History, justifies a trip here all on its own. It steeps visitors in what city life was like over the centuries, even including a substantial section about how Montréal handles the massive amounts of snow and ice it receives each year. More than 16,600 costumes, 65,000 paintings, and 1.25 million historical photographs documenting Canadian life are rotated in and out of storage to be displayed. A First Nations room features objects from Canada's native population, including

This grouse-shaped feast dish is just one of the many Canadian artifacts displayed at the Musée McCord.

meticulous beadwork, baby carriers, and fishing implements. 🕐 1½ hr. 690 rue Sherbrooke ouest. ☎ 514/398-7100. www.mccord-museum.qc.ca. Admission C$13 adults, C$10 seniors, C$7 students, C$5 children 6–12, free for children 5 and under; free admission on the first Sat of the month 10am–noon. Tues–Fri 10am–6pm, Sat–Sun 10am–5pm. June 24–Sept 1 and holiday weekends also Mon 10am–5pm. Métro: McGill.

A sketch of the historic Hochelaga Iroquois village.

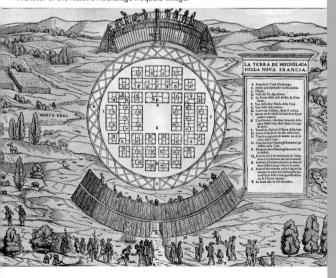

Today's First Nations

Native sovereignty and "the land question," notes prominent filmmaker Alanis Obomsawin, "have been issues since the French and English first settled the area. A lot of promises were made and never kept." A member of the Abenaki Nation who was raised on the Odanak Reserve near Montréal, Obomsawin provides unflinching looks at that tension and at the lives of contemporary Native Americans, who are referred to collectively in the Québec province as members of the First Nations. She began making movies for the National Film Board of Canada in 1967 and has produced more than 30 documentaries about the hard edges of the lives of aboriginal people. Termed "the first lady of First Nations film" by the commissioner of the film board in 2008, Obomsawin received the Governor General's Performing Arts Award for Lifetime Artistic Achievement that year.

One of her major works is *Kanehsatake: 270 Years of Resistance* (1993). It details a wrenching incident in 1990 that pitted native peoples against the government over lands about an hour west of Montréal that were slated to be turned into a golf course. The clash degenerated into a months-long armed standoff between Mohawks and authorities. "What the confrontation of 1990 showed is that this is a generation that is not going to put up with what happened in the past," says Obomsawin. Her movies are available through the National Film Board (www.nfb.ca).

The Pointe-à-Callière history museum sits on the exact location of the city's founding.

❷ Site of the Amerindian Horchelaga Settlement. On rue Sherbrooke, just to the left of the main gate of McGill University, a stone on the lawn marks the spot of the village of Hochelaga, a community of Iroquois who lived and farmed here before the first Europeans arrived. When French explorer Jacques Cartier stepped from his ship onto the land and visited Hochelaga in 1535, he noted that the village had 50 large homes, each housing several families. When the French returned in 1603, the village was empty. ⊙ *10 min. Near 845 rue Sherbrooke ouest. Métro: McGill.*

❸ ★★★ Pointe-à-Callière. Built on the very site where the original colony of Montréal was established in 1642, this modern Museum of Archaeology and History provides details on the region's inhabitants, from Amerindians to French trappers to Scottish merchants. A 16-minute multimedia show keeps the history slick and painless if a little chamber-of-commerce upbeat. ⏱ 1½ hr. See p 10, bullet ④.

Just around the corner from Pointe-à-Callière, 4️⃣ **Marché de la Villete** offers a traditional French snack or meal. It started life as an atmospheric boucherie and charcuterie market specializing in cheeses, meats, and breads, and then added a couple of tables. The staff is flirty and welcoming to the locals and waves of tourists who settle in. Try the hearty cassoulet de maison, which is packed with duck confit, pork belly, homemade sausage, and silky smooth beans, all topped with crunchy bread crumbs. *324 rue St-Paul ouest.* ☎ 514/807-8084. $$.

The museum located under the Chapelle Notre-Dame-de-Bon-Secours offers visitors a glimpse into the life of Marguerite Bourgeoys.

5️⃣ Musée du Château Ramezay. Claude de Ramezay, the colony's 11th governor, built this château as his residence in 1705. It was home to the city's royal French governors for almost 4 decades, until Ramezay's heirs sold it to a

Marguerite Bourgeoys

One of the "first women" of Montréal is Marguerite Bourgeoys (1620–1700), a teacher who traveled from France in the mid–17th century to join the nascent New France colony of 50 people. She was 33 when she arrived. A true pioneer, she built schools for both the settlers and native children, and cofounded the Congregation of Notre-Dame, Canada's first nuns' order. The settlement prospered, contained until the 1800s in the area known today as Vieux-Montréal. Bourgeoys was canonized in 1982 as the Canadian church's first female saint.

The Musée Marguerite-Bourgeoys is devoted to relating Bourgeoys' life and work. It's housed in a restored 18th-century crypt in the Chapelle Notre-Dame-de-Bon-Secours (p 65, bullet ⑨), in Vieux-Montréal. In 2005, for the chapel's 350th birthday, Marguerite's remains were brought to the church and interred in the altar.

1759: Britain Takes Québec City from France

It can't be overstated how much the British and French struggle for dominance in the 1700s and 1800s for North America—the New World—continues to shape the character of the Québec province today. A bit of history is in order. In 1607, a group of British entrepreneurs under a charter from King James I sailed west and founded the British colony of Jamestown, in what would later become Virginia. French explorer Samuel de Champlain arrived in Québec City a year later, determined to establish a French colony on the North American continent as well.

By the 1750s, the constant struggle between Britain and France for dominance in the Canadian region had escalated. The French appointed General Louis Joseph, marquis de Montcalm, to command their forces in Québec City. The British sent an expedition of 4,500 men in a fleet under the command of General James Wolfe. The British troops surprised the French by coming up and over the cliffs of Québec City's Cap Diamant, and the ensuing skirmish, fought on September 13, 1759, lasted 18 to 25 minutes, depending on whose account you read. It resulted in 600 casualties, including both generals.

The battle had a significant impact on the future of North America. Britain was victorious, and as a result, the continent remained under English influence for more than a century. That authority carries on today: Queen Elizabeth II's face graces all Canadian currency.

trading company in 1745. Fifteen years later, British conquerors took it over, and then in 1775 an army of American revolutionaries invaded Montréal and used the château as their headquarters. For 6 weeks in 1776, Benjamin Franklin spent his days here, trying to persuade the Québécois to rise with the American colonists against British rule (he failed). Exhibits about natives and the New World, the fur trade, and New France share space with old portraits, Amerindian artifacts, and other memorabilia related to the economic and social activities of the 18th and 19th centuries. ⏱ *1 hr. 280 rue Notre-Dame est.* ☎ *514/ 861-3708. www.chateauramezay. qc.ca. Admission C$9 adults, C$7*

Recreations of 18th-century life in Montréal are the prime reason to visit the Musée du Château Ramezay.

Samuel de Champlain, known as "The Father of New France," established a fur trading post where Pointe-à-Callière now stands.

seniors, C$6 students, C$4.50 children 5–17, free for children 4 and under. June to late Nov daily

10am–6pm; late Nov to May Tues–Sun 10am–4:30pm. Métro: Champ-de-Mars.

The Language of Separatism

The defining dialectic of Canadian life is culture and language, and they're thorny issues that have long threatened to tear the country apart. Many Québécois have long believed that making their province a separate, independent state is the only way to maintain their rich French culture in the face of the Anglophone (English-speaking) ocean that surrounds them. Québec's role within the Canadian federation has been the most debated and volatile topic of conversation in Canadian politics for the past 50 years. The tension is long simmering: After France lost power in Québec to the British in the 18th century, a kind of linguistic exclusionism developed, with wealthy Scottish and English bankers and merchants denying French-Canadians access to upper levels of business and government. The bias continued well into the 20th century.

The separatist movement began in earnest when René Lévesque founded the Parti Québécois (PQ) in 1968. The PQ became the governing party in 1976, and in 1977 passed Bill 101, which all but banned the use of English on public signage. French remains the state language across the Québec province, and all signs are still required to be in French.

Cultural Montréal

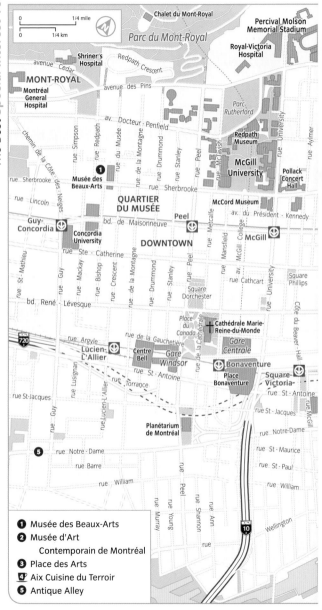

- **1** Musée des Beaux-Arts
- **2** Musée d'Art
     Contemporain de Montréal
- **3** Place des Arts
- **4** Aix Cuisine du Terroir
- **5** Antique Alley

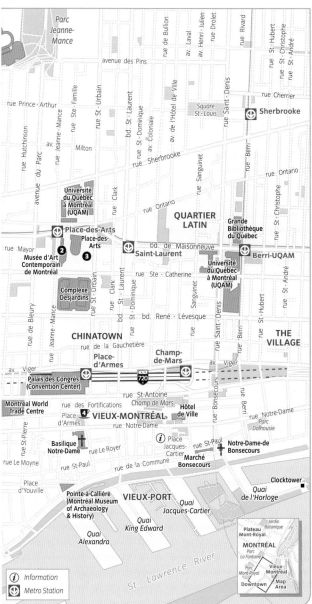

Parc Jeanne-Mance

rue de Bullion

av. Laval

av. Henri-Julien

rue Drolet

rue Rivard

rue St-Hubert

rue St-Christophe

rue St-André

avenue des Pins

rue Prince-Arthur

rue Hutchinson

avenue du Parc

av. Jeanne-Mance

rue Ste-Famille

rue St-Urbain

bd. St-Laurent

rue St-Dominique

av. Coloniale

av. de l'Hôtel de Ville

rue Cherrier

rue Saint-Denis

Sherbrooke

Square St-Louis

Milton

rue Sherbrooke

rue Berri

rue Ontario

rue Clark

rue Ontario

rue Sanguinet

rue St-Christophe

Université du Québec à Montréal (UQAM)

QUARTIER LATIN

Grande Bibliothèque du Québec

Place-des-Arts
Place-des-Arts

rue Mayor

2
Musée d'Art Contemporain de Montréal

3

Saint-Laurent
bd. de Maisonneuve

Berri-UQAM

rue St-Christophe

Université du Québec à Montréal (UQAM)

rue Ste-Catherine

rue St-Hubert

rue St-André

Complexe Desjardins

rue de Bleury

rue Jeanne-Mance

rue St-Urbain

rue Clark

bd. St-Laurent

rue St-Dominique

bd. René-Lévesque

rue Saint-Denis

rue Berri

THE VILLAGE

CHINATOWN
rue de la Gauchetière

Place-d'Armes

Champ-de-Mars

av. Viger

av. Viger

rue Bonsecours

rue Berri

Palais des Congrès (Convention Center)

720

Montréal World Trade Centre

rue des Fortifications

Place d'Armes

Champ de Mars

VIEUX-MONTRÉAL

Hôtel de Ville

rue Notre-Dame
Parc Dalhousie

rue St-Pierre

rue Notre-Dame

Basilique Notre-Dame
rue Le Royer

(i) Place Jacques-Cartier

rue St-Paul

Notre-Dame-de-Bonsecours

rue Le Moyne

rue St-Paul

rue de la Commune

Marché Bonsecours

Place d'Youville

Pointe-à-Callière (Montréal Museum of Archaeology & History)

VIEUX-PORT

Quai Jacques-Cartier

Clocktower

Quai de l'Horloge

Quai Alexandra

Quai King Edward

St. Lawrence River

Jardin Botanique

Plateau Mont-Royal

MONTRÉAL
Parc La Fontaine

Parc Mont-Royal

Downtown

Vieux-Montréal

Map Area

(i) Information

⬥ Metro Station

With comprehensive museums, a rich artistic tradition that draws from the old and the very new, and a creative music community, Montréal is Canada's cultural mecca. At the destinations highlighted here, you can sample fine art from the Renaissance, musical masterpieces, and funky galleries where everything old is new again. START: **Métro: Guy-Concordia.**

The Musée des Beaux-Arts is known primarily for its European and Canadian paintings, but also houses an excellent collection of sculpture.

❶ ★★★ Musée des Beaux-Arts. The best hunting ground for art hounds is one of Canada's most comprehensive art repositories. Included are works by prominent French-Canadian landscape watercolorist Marc-Aurèle Fortin (1888–1970), and, in the ultramodern Moshe Safdie–designed Jean-Noël Desmarais Pavilion, works by Old European masters, a number of decent Impressionist paintings (including an unusual still life by Renoir), and modern paintings by Picasso and Miró. 🕐 *2 hr. See p 13, bullet ❷.*

❷ Musée d'Art Contemporain de Montréal. The city's contemporary arts museum is devoted exclusively to the avant-garde and modern works created since 1939.

Much of the permanent collection is by Québécois artists such as Jean-Paul Riopelle, Betty Goodwin, and Paul-Émile Borduas, and recent temporary exhibitions have included the photography of Robert Polidori and the installations and looped video projections of Christine Davis. Exhibit halls are smartly arranged with photographs, canvases, and sculptures. An excellent museum boutique sells Québec-made and European products from jewelry to kids' toys. 🕐 *1 hr. 185 rue Ste-Catherine ouest. ☎ 514/847-6226. www.macm.org. Admission C$8 adults, C$6 seniors, C$4 students, free for children 11 and under, free for all Wed 6–9pm. Tues–Sun 11am–6pm (until 9pm Wed and the first Fri of most months). Métro: Place des Arts.*

❸ ★★ Place des Arts. Don your finest eveningwear and settle in for some refined entertainment. The only cultural complex of its kind in Canada, Place des Arts is similar to New York's Lincoln Center and home to five concert halls and theaters ranging from the grand to the intimate. It's here that you'll find Montréal's symphony orchestra, its opera company, and theatrical performances by other groups. During some festivals and events, the center's outdoor plaza is used as an open-air theater. *175 rue Ste-Catherine ouest. ☎ 514/842-2112. www.pda.qc.ca. Métro: Place des Arts.*

Lodged in the high-end Place d'Armes Hôtel, **❹ Aix Cuisine du Terroir** (just call it "X") is a highlight

An amuse-bouche, or premeal complimentary taste sent out from the kitchen to "amuse your mouth," of caviar with eggplant and aioli might set the course. Portions are generous enough that you could graze on a few appetizers alone. Restful tones, tan banquettes, and flickering gas lamps set an earthy, urbane mood. *See p 98.*

The Musée d'Art Contemporain de Montréal is a sure bet for thought-provoking art.

of Vieux-Montréal dining. Terroir refers to soil, and a gastronomical allegiance to products grown in the immediate region dominates, evidenced in dishes such as the roasted Québec duck breast and the veal chop from Charlevoix, the rural region north of Québec City.

⑤ **Antique Alley.** If you walk west from Vieux-Montréal on rue Notre-Dame, you'll find some of the best antiquing in the city. It's about a 45-minute walk if you don't stop. You first come to a tangle of highways, and then to some of the city's newer (and then older) condominium complexes. About 20 minutes after you've started, just after rue Guy, the gentrified Antique Alley begins. Little shops on the next few streets are chock-a-block with high- and low-end antiques. You'll eventually reach Marché Atwater, one of the city's major food and vegetable markets, and the Lionel-Groulx Métro stop. 🕐 *1½ hr. Rue Notre-Dame from about rue Guy to av. Atwater. Métro: Square Victoria to start, Lionel-Groulx to return.*

Place des Arts—Canada's top cultural complex.

Gastronomic Montréal

Metro Station

MONTRÉAL
Longueuil
Lachine
Lasalle
La Prairie

MILE END
Rosemont
Parc Père-Marquette

ch. de la Côte-Ste-Catherine

bd. St - Laurent
rue St - Denis

av. Laurier
bd. St - Joseph

Parc Sir-Wilfrid-Laurier

Papineau

Laurier

PLATEAU MONT-ROYAL

av. du Parc

Parc du Mont-Royal

av. du Parc Jeanne-Mance

Monument Sir-George-Étienne Cartier

Croix du Mont-Royal

av. du

Mont - Royal
Mont-Royal

rue Rachel

Duluth

Parc La Fontaine

av. des Pins

av. des Pins

rue Sherbrooke

Sherbrooke

Sherbrooke

McGill University

McCord Museum

rue University

Place-des-Arts

St-Laurent

QUARTIER LATIN

Berri-UQAM

Ontario

THE VILLAGE

Papineau av.

Peel

McGill

bd. de Maisonneuve

Beaudry

rue Ste - Catherine

DOWNTOWN

CHINATOWN

bd. René - Lévesque

Bonaventure

INTERNATIONAL QUARTER

Square-Victoria

Champ-de-Mars

Place-d'Armes

Palais des Congrès (Convention Center)

rue St - Antoine

rue Notre - Dame

VIEUX-MONTRÉAL

VIEUX-PORT

St. Lawrence River

Pont de la Concorde

0   1/4 mile
0   1/4 km

❶ Marché Atwater
❷ Toque!
❸ Ferreira Café
❹ Au Pied de Cochon
❺ Schwartz's
❻A St-Viateur Bagels
❻B Fairmont Bagels

Despite the prevalence of French and American influences on the local cuisine, the city's international flavor permeates the kitchens of its restaurants and the shelves of its gourmet groceries and markets. The result? Creation of many fusion foodstuffs that have become inextricable parts of the city's personality. Use every opportunity to sample the treats you find—go in with the idea that if you haven't tried it before, the time is now. START: **Métro: Lionel-Groulx.**

Marché Atwater, Montréal's best public market, sells a mouthwatering array of fresh produce and other delicacies.

1 ★ **Marché Atwater.** The Atwater market, west of Vieux-Montréal, is an indoor-outdoor farmer's

market that's open daily. French in flavor (of course), it features **boulangeries** and **fromageries**, fresh fruits, vegetables, chocolates, and flowers, and shops with food to go. Be sure to visit Première Moisson for its jewel-like pastries, artisan breads, and sublime terrines. You can walk here in about 45 minutes from Vieux-Montréal by heading west on rue Notre-Dame, or take the Métro. 🕐 *1 hr. 138 rue Atwater. Open daily. Métro: Lionel-Groulx.*

2 ★★★ **Toque!** This is, to many minds, the best restaurant in the city. Ever-questing Normand Laprise

The staff at Au Pied de Cochon prepares pork—cochon—in numerous inventive ways.

Poutine: A Tasty Mess

Though they're both essentially french fries with gravy and cheese on top, don't ever make the mistake of equating *poutine* with American "disco fries." Québécois will be quick to point out that the beauty of their beloved snack lies in the cheese: Real *poutine* uses cheese curds that don't melt completely (disco fries are usually topped with cheddar). Legend has it that the dish's name originated in 1957 when restaurateur Fernand LaChance received a request from a customer for french fries and cheese in a bag. He responded, "Ca va faire une maudite poutine!" Roughly translated: "That's going to make a damn mess!" A mess it may have been, but it also was a bona fide culinary hit, made even more so when gravy was tacked onto the recipe a few years later. Today *poutine* is a fixture on the Québec dining scene, and a must-try when you're in town. It's available both in fast-food venues and high-end restaurants, but the best place to try it is **La Banquise,** at the northwest corner of Parc La Fontaine, where there are 25 variations on the menu. See p 100.

Poutine—french fries with cheese curds and gravy—is arguably the city's favorite fast-food.

and partner Christine Lamarche keep the dazzlingly postmodern venue in a league of its own. The always-changing menu has featured cauliflower soup with foie gras shavings and milk foam, smoked suckling pig cheek with maple-water sponge toffee, and olive oil sorbet with blood orange. The restaurant is a member of the gold-standard organization Relais & Châteaux. *See p 104.*

❸ ★★★ **Ferreira Café.** In a city where French food and its derivations rule, the lush orange and blue Mediterranean decor at this Portuguese restaurant and its big, fleshy mounds of grilled squid and black cod create an experience that is downright sexy. Another highlight:

Cataplana, a fragrant stew of mussels, clams, potatoes, shrimp, *chouriço* sausage, and chunks of cod and

The legendary Schwartz's is renowned for its smoked meat.

Fairmount Bagels serves up more than 20 varieties of Montréal's most renowned baked goods every day.

salmon. A late-night menu for C\$24 is available daily from 10pm. *See p 100.*

4 ★★ **Au Pied de Cochon.** Packed to the walls 6 nights per week, this Plateau restaurant is a cult favorite. The PDC's Cut, a slab of pork weighing in at more than a pound, is emblematic. Chef Martin Picard gets particularly clever with one ingredient: foie gras. It comes in 10 combinations, including a goofy creation called Duck in a Can which does, indeed, arrive with a can opener. When you feel like another bite will send you into a cholesterol-induced coma, sugar pie *(tarte au sucre)* is the only fitting finish. *See p 98.*

5 ★★★ **Schwartz's.** Housed in a long, narrow storefront, with a lunch counter and simple tables and chairs crammed impossibly close to each other, this is as nondescript a culinary landmark as you'll find. French-first language laws turned the official name of this old-time Jewish delicatessen into "Chez Schwartz Charcuterie Hébraïque de Montréal," but everyone calls it Schwartz's. There's usually a line to get in, and most people order sandwiches plates that come heaped with its famed smoked meat (*viande fumée*—a kind of brisket) and piles of rye bread. A take-out window opened in 2008 in honor of the restaurant's 80th birthday. *See p 103.*

★★ **6A** **St-Viateur Bagels** & **6B** **Fairmont Bagels.** The unique texture and delicious, honey-tinged flavor of Montréal bagels warrant not one, but a pair of entries on this tour—the giants who battle it out every year for the title of Best Bagel in the City. St-Viateur uses wood-burning ovens and old-fashioned baking techniques brought from eastern Europe by founder Myer Lewkowicz. Fairmont, open 24 hours 7 days a week, offers greater variety, with 20 options including mueslix and (shudder) blueberry. Compare a classic plain or sesame and be the ultimate arbiter yourself. *See p 103.*

Romantic Montréal

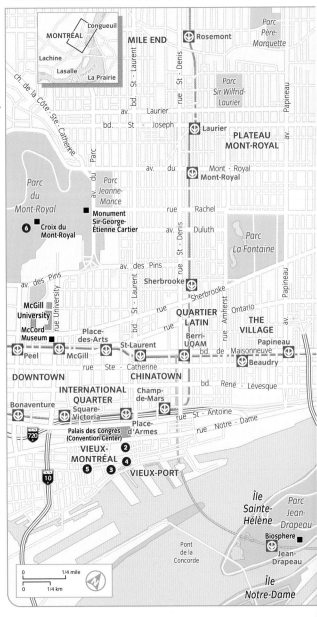

MONTRÉAL
Longueuil
Lachine
Lasalle
La Prairie
St Lawrence

MILE END
Rosemont
Parc Père-Marquette

Parc Sir-Wilfrid-Laurier

av. Laurier
bd. St - Joseph
Laurier
PLATEAU MONT-ROYAL

ch. de la Côte-Ste-Catherine

av. du
Mont - Royal
Mont-Royal

Parc du Mont-Royal

Parc Jeanne-Mance

rue Rachel
Parc La Fontaine

Monument Sir-George-Étienne Cartier

Croix du Mont-Royal

av. Duluth

av. des Pins

Sherbrooke
Sherbrooke

McGill University

QUARTIER LATIN

THE VILLAGE

McCord Museum

Place-des-Arts

Berri-UQAM

Papineau

Peel
McGill
St-Laurent

Beaudry

rue Ste - Catherine

CHINATOWN

DOWNTOWN

bd. René - Lévesque

Bonaventure

INTERNATIONAL QUARTER

Square-Victoria

Champ-de-Mars

Place-d'Armes

rue St - Antoine

rue Notre - Dame

Palais des Congrès (Convention Center)

720

VIEUX-MONTRÉAL

2

10

5

3

4

VIEUX-PORT

Île Sainte-Hélène

Parc Jean-Drapeau

Biosphere

Jean-Drapeau

Pont de la Concorde

Île Notre-Dame

0   1/4 mile
0   1/4 km

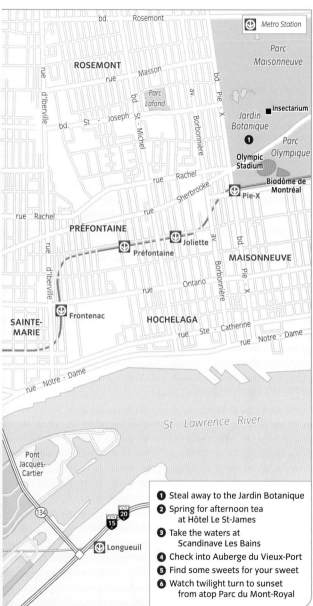

1 Steal away to the Jardin Botanique
2 Spring for afternoon tea
   at Hôtel Le St-James
3 Take the waters at
   Scandinave Les Bains
4 Check into Auberge du Vieux-Port
5 Find some sweets for your sweet
6 Watch twilight turn to sunset
   from atop Parc du Mont-Royal

Romance is in the eyes of the beholder, which makes this the trickiest tour to propose. Sitting hand in hand on a quiet park bench might be all you need for a moment to be luminous— while your best friend might dream of having a partner drop C$300 on a luxurious dinner in a sky-high restaurant. Options here range from the modest to the opulent. START: **Métro: Pie-IX.**

❶ Steal away to the Jardin Botanique. You'll be hard-pressed to find an area within the botanical gardens that isn't conducive to cuddling. The Japanese Garden has an extremely relaxing Zen garden, while the butterfly house hosts hundreds of live butterflies who flit around and sometimes alight on visitors' shoulders. And the Chinese Garden has pavilions and inner courtyards to tuck away into. ⏱ *1½ hr. See p 21, bullet* ❾.

❷ Spring for afternoon tea at Hôtel Le St-James. The most lavish of Montréal's hotels serves tea from 2:30 to 5pm in its grand hall. Scones, blood orange marmalade, petits fours, fresh berries, and the world's best teas are available. At C$30 or C$45 a serving it's not cheap, but you're trying to impress, right? ⏱ *1½ hr. See p 129.*

❸ Take the waters at Scandinave Les Bains. Bath complexes

The antiques-filled Hôtel Le St-James is quite luxurious.

are common throughout Scandinavia, but less so in North America. This center in Vieux-Montréal, which opened in 2009, offers Euro-style relaxation through water. Visitors wear bathing suits and have the run of the complex. There's a warm bath the size of a small swimming

The beautiful Jardin Botanique is the perfect spot for a romantic stroll.

Taking in the waters at La Spa Scandinave is a great way to unwind with your special someone.

pool, with jets and a waterfall. There's a steam room thick with eucalyptus oil scent, and a Finnish-style dry sauna. Peppered throughout the hallways are sling-back chairs for napping. ⏱ *2+ hr. 71 rue de la Commune ouest.* ☎ *514/288-2009. www.scandinave.com. Admission C$42. Open daily 10am–10pm. Métro: Champ-de-Mars.*

❹ Check into Auberge du Vieux-Port. Exposed brick and stone walls, massive beams, and polished hardwood floors define the hideaway bedrooms, many of which offer unobstructed views of Vieux-Port. In the late afternoon, guests get a complimentary glass of wine with cheese in the small wine bar off the lobby, with live jazz adding to the mood Thursday through Saturday starting at 6:30pm. *See p 127.*

❺ Find some sweets for your sweet. Perhaps cupcakes from the cute shop Les Glaceurs in Vieux-Montréal? Or maybe treats by local chocolatier Les Chocolats de Chloé, which spices up offerings with cardamom, buckwheat honey, and Espelette pepper? (The chocolates are sold out of a shop in the Plateau and at the Vieux-Montréal restaurant Olive et Gourmando.) *See p 59, 88, and 103.*

❻ Watch twilight turn to sunset from atop Parc Mont-Royal. The lookouts along rue Camillien-Houde and the front terrace of the Chalet du Mont-Royal at the top of the small mountain called Mont-Royal offer the most popular panoramic view of Montréal and the St-Lawrence River. There are a web of options for trekking the small mountain (see our suggested walk in chapter 3), or you can take a cab, a bus, or your own car. *See p 80, bullet* ❻.

The charming rooms at Auberge du Vieux-Port are popular with couples.

High Design Montréal

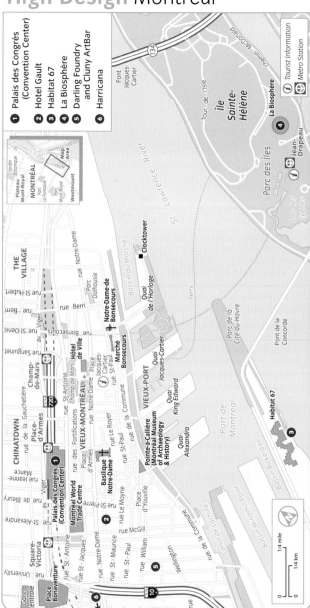

1 Palais des Congrès (Convention Center)
2 Hotel Gault
3 Habitat 67
4 La Biosphère
5 Darling Foundry and Cluny ArtBar
6 Harricana

i Tourist Information
Metro Station

M ontréal is one of North America's most stylish cities, and the municipality has worked in recent years to capitalize on that appeal to entice artists to create and art-minded travelers to visit. In 2006, it became the first North American city to be appointed a UNESCO City of Design. If you're here in May, be sure to take in the Design Montréal Open House, a 2-day free event when creative agencies, projects, and sites throw open their doors to the public. Details are at www.designmontreal.com. Here are some highlights to take in, in and around Vieux-Montréal. **START: Métro: Place d'Armes.**

Hôtel Gault merges stylish modern design with industrial architecture.

❶ Palais des Congrès (Convention Center). A convention center as design triumph? As unlikely as that seems, yes. Transparent glass exterior walls are a crazy quilt of pink, yellow, blue, green, red, and purple rectangles. Step into the inside hallway for the full effect— when the sun streams in, it's like being inside a huge kaleidoscope. The walls went up from 2000 to 2002 as part of renovation and extension of the center and are the vision of Montréal architect Mario Saia. ⏱ *15 min. 201 ave Viger ouest.* ☎ *514/ 871-8122. www.congresmtl.com. Métro: Place d'Armes.*

❷ Hôtel Gault. Vieux-Montréal's rich character derives from the careful reuse of industrial buildings. Why tear down beauty just to put up more of the same old, same old? For this hotel, which opened in 2002, interior designer Atelier YH2 and architect Paul Bernier left the monumental concrete walls of a 19th-century textile warehouse raw and added brushed-steel work surfaces for a chic, contemporary feel. As one journalist noted, "Hôtel Gault caters to exactly the sort of guest who might choose lodging based on the provenance of the furniture, and exemplifies the ways in which Montréal has been, like other cities

The Biosphère is home to a number of multimedia exhibitions on ecological issues.

around the world, reinventing itself to attract a certain breed of urban sophisticate." The sleek lobby, with its massive arched windows, also functions as a bar/cafe/breakfast area, and the Gault Restaurant invites all to come and play. ⏲ *30 min. See p 129.*

❸ Habitat 67. In 1967, Montréal hosted the World's Fair, which it called Expo 67. It was hugely successful—62 nations participated and over 50 million people visited— and overnight, Montréal was a star. Its avant-garde vision was on display, and it became a kind of prototype for a 20th-century city. One of

the most exhilarating buildings built for display was Habitat 67, a 158-unit housing complex on the St. Lawrence River facing Vieux-Montréal. Designed by Montréal architect Moshe Safdie, it looks like a collection of module concrete blocks, all piled together and interconnected. The vision was to show what affordable, community housing could be. Today it's higher-end housing and not open to the public. But it can be seen from the western end of Vieux-Port, and photos and information can be found at Safdie's website, www.msafdie.com. ⏲ *30 min. View from corner of rue St-Pierre and rue de la Commune in Vieux-Port.*

❹ La Biosphère. Geodesic domes popped up across the world's landscape during the 20th century for industrial and even residential use. This building, located on Île Ste-Hélène near to Vieux-Montréal, was designed by American architect Buckminster Fuller to serve as the American Pavilion for Expo 67. A fire destroyed the sphere's acrylic skin in 1976, and for almost 20 years it served no purpose other than as a harbor landmark. In 1995, Environment Canada (www.ec.gc.ca) joined with the city

Montréal Fashion Week

Fashion simmers in this city, where innovative locals are making international names for themselves. Montréal Fashion Week, held in both March and October, is the best place to take it all in. Runway shows go up at Marché Bonsecours in Vieux-Montréal (p 65), with a designer showroom and end-of-event sample sale in the same space. Montréal designer Denis Gagnon (www.denis gagnon.ca) is a regular star at the event. Show details: www.montreal fashionweek.ca. A city map of designer venues: www.montreal fashionmap.com.

Cluny ArtBar, located in a former foundry, is a great place to grab a bite.

of Montréal to convert the space, and it's now an interactive science facility devoted to promoting awareness of the St. Lawrence–Great Lakes ecosystem. ⏱ *2 hr. 160 chemin Tour-de-l'Isle (Île Ste-Hélène).* ☎ *514/283-5000. www.biosphere. ec.gc.ca. Admission C$10 adults, C$8 seniors and students 18 and over, free for children 17 and under. Métro: Parc Jean-Drapeau.*

⑤ Darling Foundry and Cluny ArtBar. Artists and high-tech businesses are moving into the loft-and-factory district west of avenue McGill, at the edge of Vieux-Montréal, though the streets are still pretty quiet here. Among the pioneers is the Darling Foundry, an avant-garde exhibition space in a vast, raw, former foundry. It showcases modern art with the mission of supporting emerging artists living and working in the heart of the city. Cluny is a breakfast and lunch spot that's open Monday through Wednesday and Friday, 8:30am to 5pm, and Thursday until 10pm. ⏱ *30 min. See p 98.*

⑥ Harricana. One of Montréal's most prominent fashion designers takes a unique cue from the city's long history with the fur trade.

Mariouche Gagné, who was born on Île d'Orléans near Québec City in 1971, recycles old fur into funky patchwork garments and uses the slogan "Made from your mother's old coat." She also recycles silk scarves, turning them into tops and skirts. A leader in the so-called ecoluxe movement, she was one of 20 Canadian designers featured at the March 2009 Montréal Fashion Week. ⏱ *30 min. See p 87.*

Harricana has a vast selection of stylish recycled fur apparel.

Hipster Montréal

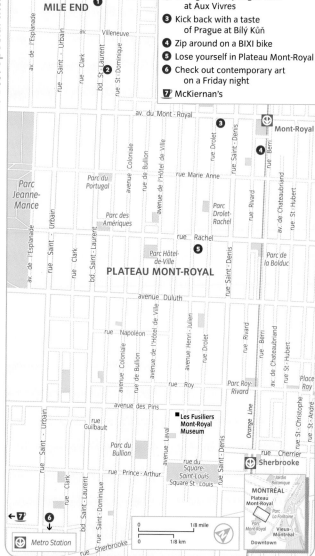

1 Stop by the sister venues Casa del Popolo and La Sala Rosa
2 Indulge in tasty vegan food at Aux Vivres
3 Kick back with a taste of Prague at Bílý Kůň
4 Zip around on a BIXI bike
5 Lose yourself in Plateau Mont-Royal
6 Check out contemporary art on a Friday night
7 McKiernan's

Where do all the hipsters hang out? A lot are in the northern reaches of Plateau Mont-Royal and into Mile End, the neighborhood a little more north still. Here you'll find boys in skinny jeans with wallet chains, girls in leggings and thrift-store finds, and both genders in tight blue jean jackets, geeking out and creating wildly. Here's a sample day, starting at one of the most important venues for the independent music scene in the city.

START: **Métro: Laurier.**

① Stop by the sister venues Casa del Popolo and La Sala Rosa.

Spanish for "The House of the People," the cozy Casa del Popolo is set in a scruffy storefront and serves vegetarian food, operates a laid-back bar complete with ratty couches, and has a small first-floor stage. For many it's a refuge from the trendier, more expensive venues farther south on boulevard St-Laurent. Across the street, sister performance space La Sala Rosa is a terrific music venue and has a full calendar of interesting offerings from around the city and beyond. ⏱ *30 min. See p 113 and 114.*

The bustling Aux Vivres is a popular spot for health- and eco-conscious diners.

② Indulge in tasty vegan food at Aux Vivres.

In business since 1997, Aux Vivres has been humming and busy since moving into its current location in 2006. It's a restaurant with white Formica tables, raw blonde walls, and pink Chinese lanterns, and there's a juice bar off to one side and a back terrace. All foods are vegan, all vegetables are organic, and all tofu and tempeh are local. ⏱ *1 hr. See p 98.*

Casa del Popolo serves vegetarian food in a laid-back setting.

Quirky and hip, Bílý Kůň is a great place to grab a drink after exploring the surrounding shops.

❸ Kick back with a taste of Prague at Bílý Kůň. Exuding a relaxed cool, Bílý Kůň brings in students and professionals who sit elbow to elbow at small tables. The room is lit by candles at night, and in summer twirling ceiling fans and picture windows open to the street. Decor is quirky (hello, mounted ostrich heads) and there are several absinthe drink options. Open daily from 3pm to 3am, it offers live jazz from 6 to 8pm daily and DJs most nights. If you're visiting in the day, build in time to stop by the little shops along the same street. There's lots of used clothing and kitschy stuff, and Aime Com Moi, at 150 av. Mont-Royal est, features fabulously funky dresses by Québécois designers. ⏱ *2 hr. See p 110.*

❹ Zip around on a BIXI bike. In 2009, the city initiated a long-awaited self-service bicycle rental program called BIXI, an abbreviated combination of the words *bicyclette* and *taxi.* It's similar to programs in Berlin, Paris, and Barcelona. Users pick up BIXI bikes from designated stands throughout the city and drop them off at any other stand, for a small fee. Some 3,000 bikes were to be in operation by the end of 2009 with some 300 stations in Montréal's central boroughs. ⏱ *1 hr. Stands are located throughout the city, including at Métro Mont-Royal. Fees and details are listed at www. bixi.com/home.*

❺ Lose yourself in Plateau Mont-Royal. What, like, just walk with no agenda? *Naturellement!* Whether its tree-lined streets are littered with gold and scarlet leaves in the fall or fresh snow in the winter, this neighborhood is perfect for a leisurely stroll. Sit tête-à-tête at a cafe on rue St-Denis or head to the boutiques and bars on avenue du Mont-Royal or make it up as you go

The Plateau is one of Montréal's most picturesque and romantic neighborhoods.

Plateau Mont-Royal is home to numerous trendy boutiques.

along—a destination-free day is the best way to get into the neighborhood's flow. ⏱ *2 hr. Area bordered by rues St-Urbain and Papineau and rues Sherbrooke to Laurier. Métro: Mont-Royal.*

⑥ Check out contemporary art on a Friday night. On Friday Nocturnes—the first Friday of most months—the Musée d'Art Contemporain de Montréal stays open until 9pm with live music, bar service, and tours of the exhibition galleries. The museum always has temporary exhibitions up, while its permanent collection includes works by international figures Sam Taylor-Wood, Nan Goldin, Richard Serra, and Bruce Nauman. ⏱ *2 hr. See p 32.*

If you're sporting sleeve tattoos, cute little vintage clothes, or a C$200 haircut designed to look like you just fell out of bed, head south and west to **⑦ McKiernan's luncheonette and wine bar,** where chainsaws and Spam tins form the decor. This cramped outcropping not far from the Atwater market may feel inhospitable to persons not dressed like rock stars, but the food is inventive and reasonably priced. A poulet rôti tikka sandwich with two chutneys marries all the right flavors, as does the shrimpy dog—a shrimp, caper, and pickle mixture served cold in two grilled flatbread buns. *2485 rue Notre-Dame ouest av. du Parc.* ☎ *514/759-6677. $$.*

Montréal's Parks

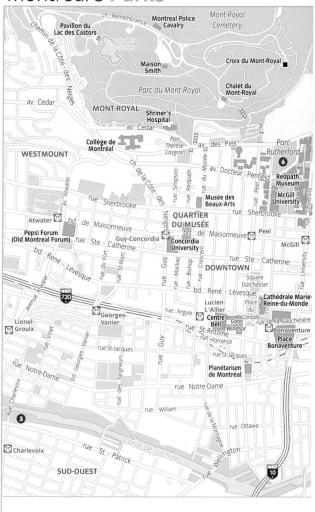

❶ Poke around Vieux-Port
❷ Bike or blade the
   Lachine Canal bike path
❸ Getting in the water
❹ Take in the Tam Tams

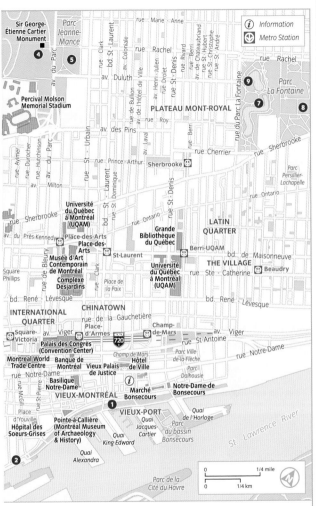

5 Leap onto the beach volleyball courts

6 Find some pick-up Frisbee

7 Do some paddle boating

8 Hit the tennis courts

9 Plan a night at Théâtre de Verdure

Shopping, eating, spending, drinking—sometimes all that consuming gets to be just a little much. When you're looking to simply hang out in some green space, or hit the water, or go for a bike ride, make like a Montréaler. Here are three great parks and some popular ways to take them in.

Vieux-Port & Lachine Canal

Montréal's Old Port—called Vieux-Port in French—was transformed in 1992 from a dreary commercial wharf area into a promenade and public park with bicycle paths, exhibition halls, and a variety of family activities. It stretches along the waterfront parallel to rue de la Commune from rue Berri in the east to rue McGill in the west. The Lachine Canal bike path starts right at rue McGill.

❶ Poke around Vieux-Port.

The port area really isn't that big— 2km (1¼-mile) long, and 53 hectares (131 acres) in all. A fun option is to rent a quadricycle from **Quadricycle** (☎ 514/849-9953; www.quadricycleintl.com), or a Q-cycle, a 4-wheeled bike-buggy that can hold two to six people. You can only ride them along Vieux-Port. The rental booth is in the heart of the

Cycling the Lachine Canal Bike Path is one of Montréal's best outdoor experiences.

waterfront area, next to the **Centre des Sciences de Montréal,** and the cost is C$15 for a three seater and C$30 for a six seater. At the same spot, you can hop onboard the open-sided **La Balade,** a small, motorized tram. It manages to find enough places to go and enough things to say to fill a 50-minute guided tour of the area (C$5 for adults). At the port's far eastern end, in the last of the old warehouses, the 1922 clock tower, **La Tour de l'Horloge,** can be climbed for free. It has 192 steps that lead past exposed clockworks to observation decks overlooking the St. Lawrence River.

Climb to the top of La Tour de l'Horloge in Vieux-Port and you'll be treated to a spectacular view of the city.

❷ Bike or blade the Lachine Canal bike path. ÇaRoule/

Montréal on Wheels (27 rue de la Commune est; ☎ 877/866-0633 or 514/866-0633; www.caroule montreal.com), on the waterfront road bordering Vieux-Port, rents bicycles and rollerblades from March

Enjoy the Outdoors, Come Snow or Come Shine

After long winters, locals pour outside to get sun and warm air at every possible opportunity. But there's lots to do when there's snow on the ground, too. And even if you arrive without your regular outdoor gear, it's easy to join in.

In warm weather, biking and rollerblading are hugely popular (see "Tap Your Own Pedal Power," p 161). Hikers and joggers take to Parc Mont-Royal and the city streets. And getting onto the water is big. In addition to kayaking on the Lachine Canal (see earlier), a popular option is taking a cruise on the St. Lawrence River. Trips are available from mid-May to mid-October, with companies such as **Le Bateau-Mouche** (☎ 800/361-9952 or 514/849-9952; www.bateau-mouche.com) and **Croisières AML Cruises** (☎ 800/563-4643 or 514/842-3871; www.croisieresaml.com) offering 60-minute, 90-minute, and evening trips. Adult fares start at C$23, and the boats leave from the piers in Vieux-Port.

In winter, cross-country skiers take advantage of the extensive course at Parc Mont-Royal (although you have to bring your own equipment). Outdoor skating rinks are set up in Vieux-Port and at Lac des Castors (Beaver Lake) in Parc Mont-Royal, with skate rentals available at both locales.

to November. Rentals are C$9 per hour and C$30 per day on weekends. The staff can set you up with a map (also downloadable from their website) and point you toward the peaceful Lachine Canal, a nearly flat 11km (6.8-mile) bicycle path that travels alongside locks and over small bridges. The path is open year-round and maintained by Parks Canada from mid-April to the end of October.

The bike shop also offers a **3-hour bicycling tour** that goes from Vieux-Port through the Quartier Latin up to Parc La Fontaine and then west to Parc Mont-Royal, south through the business district, and back into Vieux-Montréal. The cost is C$49. The tour is offered several days a week starting at 9am, with reservations required.

❸ **Don't just look at the water—get in it.** Rent kayaks, large Rabaska canoes, pedal boats,

Scenic Beaver Lake is a popular spot for outdoor enthusiasts year-round.

Relaxing by a lake in Parc La Fontaine is the perfect way to while away a summer afternoon.

or small ecofriendly electric boats about 4km (2½ miles) down the canal. **H2O Adventures** (☎ 877/935-2925 or 514/842-1306; www.h2oadventures.com) won a 2007 Grand Prix du tourisme Québécois award for its operation. Rentals start at C$8 per hour and options include a 2-hour introductory kayak lesson for C$39 on weekdays, C$45 on weekends. If you don't want to bike or walk there, take the Métro to Lionel-Groulx and head south to the canal. You'll pass the **Marché Atwater,** one of the city's premiere markets, where you can pick up food from the *boulangerie* and *fromagerie* or from any of the many prepared food shops.

Parc du Mont-Royal

Take a look at the map and suggested walk of Parc Mont-Royal on p 76. That will give you your bearings on how to get into and around the 200-hectare (494-acre) park and a feel for some of the walking highlights. Here are some additional ways to enjoy the park and its environs.

❹ **Take in the Tam Tams.** If you have a Sunday to spare from early May to late September, try out this enormous gathering of hippies, musicians, vendors, and fantasy combatants. Tam Tams attracts a few hundred drummers who

congregate late in the morning around the statue of Sir George-Etienne Cartier near avenue du Parc at the corner rue Rachel, on the park's far eastern side. The only qualification is that you have some instrument you can bang on. As the mass of random percussionists builds around the steps of the statue, the rest of the park fills with sunbathers and picnickers who turn the impromptu concert into a festive social event. You'll also find vendors hawking homemade jewelry and art, and kooky LARPers (Live Action Role Players) putting on whimsical faux battles with foam weapons in a grove of trees to the north. *Inside Parc Mont-Royal at av. du Parc and rue Rachel.*

❺ **Leap onto the beach volleyball courts or the ice rink at Parc Jeanne-Mance.** If you'd rather break a sweat, check out the park across from avenue du Parc, near where the Tam Tams set up. You'll find a baseball field, tennis courts, a football/soccer field and, best of all, beach volleyball courts. When the weather is acceptable, these giant sandboxes are full of shirtless men and bikini-clad women setting and spiking. Cold weather brings an excellent ice rink that's popular among shinny hockey players who do without full padding and play just with gloves, skates, and sticks. Even when it's −40°C (−40°F) you can still find die-hards at it. *Inside Parc Jeanne-Mance at av. du Parc and rue Duluth.*

6 Find some pick-up Frisbee in Parc Rutherford. Just south of where the walking tour of Park Mont-Royal (p 76) begins is Parc Rutherford, an enormous expanse of grass known to locals as the Réservoir. Adjacent to McGill, it's where students come to study on warm days. It's also one of the best spots for finding an ultimate Frisbee game: The university's club team practices and plays here, but you'll likely find pick-up games on other days. *Rue McTavish and av. des Pins.*

Parc La Fontaine
Many locals come to this green oasis to play in its two lakes or take in a free show in the park's outdoor theater. Many come simply to find some quiet among the flower beds that bloom bright: Some of the landscaping is done in a formal French manner, and some in a more casual English style.

7 Do some paddle boating in summer or ice skating in winter. In warm weather, waterfowl float aimlessly in the two man-made ponds set in the middle of Parc La Fontaine. Humans like to take to the water here as well, and there's nothing more peaceful than renting a paddle boat and floating lazily in the sun. When the water freezes over in winter, folks bring their caps and ice skates for some aerobic activity on the lit, music-filled rinks. Skates can be rented from a lakeside kiosk.

8 Tennis, anyone? The 14 courts here are in decent condition and are the most convenient option in downtown Montréal for tennis enthusiasts. They're lit and stay open until 10pm, and can sometimes get crowded, but try to score an evening session if you can. With the often-oppressive summer humidity, playing is far more comfortable in the cooler Montréal nights. Reservations aren't required, but to make sure you get the slot you want you'll either have to sign up at the courts in person or call ahead of time. ☎ *514/872-3626. East side of Parc La Fontaine.*

9 Plan a night at Théâtre de Verdure. Sunset does not send park visitors heading for the exits. Instead, many stay after dark because of this excellent, open-air theater—one of the best places to see a show in all of Montréal. Summer evenings almost always feature some form of free entertainment: concerts, French films, ballet performances, or tango dancing. You can pack a bottle of shiraz and a picnic basket and have a wonderfully relaxing dinner as you take it all in under the night sky. The only frustration is that the theater doesn't have a website, making it difficult for visitors to make plans in advance. Call the city's Infotouriste Centre for updates. ☎ *877/266-5687 or 514/873-2015. West end of Parc La Fontaine.*

Free summer evening performances attract throngs to the Théâtre de Verdure.

Montréal with Kids

MONTRÉAL

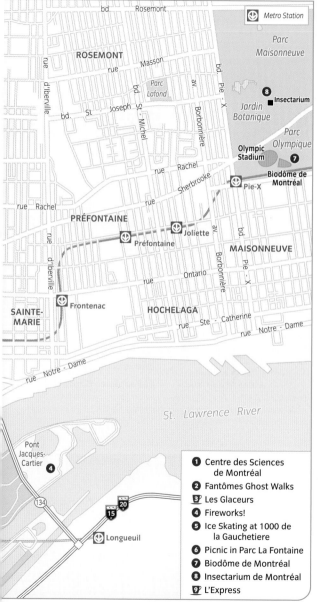

bd. Rosemont

ROSEMONT

Masson

rue

rue d'Iberville

Parc Lafond

bd. St Joseph St-Michel

bd.

Parc Maisonneuve

🔿 Metro Station

av. Pie - X

Borbonnière

bd. Pie - X

Jardin Botanique

■ Insectarium ⑧

rue Rachel

Parc Olympique

Olympic Stadium

⑦

Biodôme de Montréal

Sherbrooke

rue

🔿 Pie-X

PRÉFONTAINE

rue

🔿 Joliette

av.

🔿 Préfontaine

MAISONNEUVE

bd. Pie - X

rue Rachel

rue d'Iberville

Ontario

Borbonnière

rue

🔿 Frontenac

HOCHELAGA

SAINTE-MARIE

rue Ste - Catherine

rue Notre - Dame

rue Notre - Dame

St. Lawrence River

Pont Jacques-Cartier

④

(134)

15 20

🔿 Longueuil

① Centre des Sciences de Montréal

② Fantômes Ghost Walks

③ Les Glaceurs

④ Fireworks!

⑤ Ice Skating at 1000 de la Gauchetiere

⑥ Picnic in Parc La Fontaine

⑦ Biodôme de Montréal

⑧ Insectarium de Montréal

⑨ L'Express

Montréal is as much a playground for children as it is for adults. A good number of the city's museums and attractions tailor exhibits and activities to the city's tiniest sightseers, and parents are sure to hear hours of giddy shrieks and astonished gasps at the spots listed below. Children who speak French or are learning French might like a guidebook of their own, and for them, look for the fun *Mon Premier Guide de Voyage au Québec* (Ulysse, 2009). It's got 96 pages of photos, miniessays, and activities for kids ages 6 to 12, and can be found in provincial bookshops. START: **Métro: Place d'Armes or Champs-de-Mars.**

❶ ★ Centre des Sciences de Montréal. Running the length of a central pier in Vieux-Port (Old Port), this ambitious science center got a big overhaul in 2007. Attractions include interactive displays, multimedia challenges, and a popular IMAX theater (p 120). Designed to bring to life the concepts of 21st-century communications, energy conservation, and the life sciences, the center's extensive use of computers and electronic visual displays is particularly appealing to youngsters. Indeed, the whole place is designed for ages 9 to 14. Admission fees vary according to the combination of exhibits and movie showings you choose. To avoid long lines, preorder tickets for special exhibits. Several on-site cafes sell sandwiches, salads, and sweets. ⏲ 2 hr. Quai King Edward (Vieux-Port). ☎ 877/496-4724 or 514/496-4724. www.montrealsciencecentre.com. Open Mon–Fri 9am–4pm,

The Planetarium de Montréal screens impressive light shows that usually enthrall older kids.

Sat–Sun 10am–5pm. Call or check website for IMAX theater schedule. Admission for exhibitions C$12 adults, C$11 seniors and children 13–17, C$9 children 4–12, free for children 3 and under. Métro: Place d'Armes or Champ-de-Mars.

❷ Fantômes Ghost Walks. Evenings at 8:30, join with other intrepid souls for a ghost walk of Vieux-Montréal. The 90-minute tour

Kids love the hands-on exhibits at the Centre des Sciences de Montréal.

The spectacular International Fireworks Competition is held each summer in Montréal.

heads down back alleys and to places where gruesome events occurred and actors dress as phantoms to tell about the historical crimes of the city. Because the stories include tales of sorcery, hangings, and being burned and tortured, it's probably too scary for younger children. ⏱ 1½ hr. *360 rue St-François-Xavier.* ☎ *514/868-0303.* www.fantommontreal.com. *Admission C$23 adults, C$19 students, C$14 children 12 and under. Various evenings July–Oct 8:30pm; call or visit website for exact days. Métro: Place d'Armes.*

Can we all agree that the rise in cupcake shops is one of the greatest phenomena of the early 21st century? ③ **Les Glaceurs,** a cheery cafe with pink and lime-green walls, sells cupcakes for C$3 in flavors such as coconut, key lime, choco menthe, and strawberry. You can also pick up ice cream made by Montréal favorite Bilboquet and sandwiches. It is open daily from 11am to 6pm. *453 rue St-Sulpice (across the street from Basilique Notre-Dame).* ☎ *514/504-1469.* $.

④ ★ **Fireworks!** On 11 Saturdays from June to August, La Ronde Amusement Park hosts a huge

fireworks competition, L'International Des Feux Loto-Québec (www.internationaldesfeuxloto-quebec.com). Although the pyrotechnics can be enjoyed for free from almost anywhere in the city overlooking the river, tickets can be purchased to watch from an open-air theater at La Ronde. Tickets include entrance to the park, which features 13 rides in the "max thrill" category and an ample selection for young children, including the Tchou Tchou Train and tasses magiques, where kids sit in giant rotating tea cups. La Ronde is at Parc Jean-Drapeau on Île Ste-Hélène. ☎ *514/397-2000.* www.laronde.com. *Admission C$39 for patrons 1.37m (54 in.) or taller, C$26 for patrons shorter than 1.37m (54 in.) and for seniors, free for children 2 and under.*

⑤ ★ **Ice skating downtown.** Escape the city's stifling heat or freezing cold at this year-round rink downtown. Oddly shaped with two large columns stuck in the middle, the cozy rink is surrounded by plenty of eateries and has skate rentals on-site. Tiny Tot Mornings, typically Saturday and Sunday from 10:30 to 11:30am, are reserved for children 12 and younger and their

Skaters flock to the ice rink at 1000 rue de la Gauchetiere.

parents for their enjoyment. ⏱ *1 hr. 1000 rue de la Gauchetiere ouest.* ☎ *514/395-0555. www.le1000.com. Admission: C$6 adults, C$5 seniors and students, C$4 children 12 and under. Skate rental C$5.50. Daily 11:30am–6pm or later. Métro: Bonaventure.*

Pack up gourmet cheeses and baguettes for the adults and whatever the kids will need for a ⑥ **picnic in Parc La Fontaine.** The Plateau's gorgeous green space has scenic ponds on the quaint English (west) half and dreamy garden paths in the distinctly French (east) side. The park is a microcosm of Montréal, from its bilingual nature to its laid-back atmosphere. ⏱ *1 hr. Rue Sherbrooke and av. du Parc La Fontaine. Métro: Sherbrooke.*

⑦ ★★★ **Biodôme de Montréal.** Great fun for all ages, from young kids to teens to adults. Four ecosystems are re-created in this unusual attraction, and all have accurate temperatures, flora, and fauna. The rainforest and polar environments are the biggest hits with the littlest ones—penguins and macaws apparently have an innate ability to mesmerize children for hours. Once the

This mantis is just one of the many creepies and crawlies you'll encounter at the Insectarium de Montréal.

kids have gotten tired of watching the animals, they can try out Naturalia, a hands-on activity room. ⏱ *2 hr.* See p 20, bullet ⑧.

⑧ ★ **Insectarium de Montréal.** Live exhibits featuring scorpions, tarantulas, honey bees, ants, hissing cockroaches, and other "misunderstood creatures, which are so often wrongly feared and despised," as the Insectarium's website puts it, are displayed in this two-level structure near the rue Sherbrooke gate of the Jardin Botanique (Botanical Garden; p 21). Alongside the live creepy critters are thousands of mounted ones, including butterflies, beetles, scarabs, maggots, locusts, and giraffe weevils. Plans call for the museum to be closed for renovations for several months in early 2011, so call or check online for updated information. ⏱ *1½ hr. 4581 rue Sherbrooke est.* ☎ *514/872-1400. www.ville. montreal.qc.ca/insectarium. Open Jan 1–May 14 Tues–Sun 9am–5pm; May 15–Sept 9 daily 9am–6pm; Sept 10–Oct 31 daily 9am–9pm; Nov 1– Dec 31 Tues–Sun 9am–5pm. Admission to both Insectarium and Jardin Botanique May 15–Oct C$16.50 adults, C$12.50 seniors and students, C$8.25 children 5–17, C$2.50 children 2–4, free for children under 2; rates slightly lower Nov–mid May.*

Kids will love the crepes at ⑨ **L'Express,** this most classic of Parisian-style bistros. Popular dishes also include the ravioli maison, which are round pasta pockets filled with a flavorful mixture of beef, pork, and veal, and the croque-monsieur. *See p 102.* ●

Vieux-Montréal

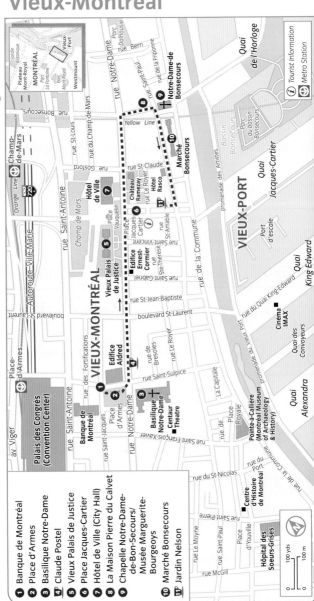

1 Banque de Montréal
2 Place d'Armes
3 Basilique Notre-Dame
4 Claude Postel
5 Vieux Palais de Justice
6 Place Jacques-Cartier
7 Hôtel de Ville (City Hall)
8 La Maison Pierre du Calvet
9 Chapelle Notre-Dame-de-Bon-Secours/Musée Marguerite-Bourgeoys
10 Marché Bonsecours
17 Jardin Nelson

Previous page: The Maisonneuve Monument and Basilique Notre-Dame in Place d'Armes.

Many cities are best explored on foot, and Montréal is one of North America's most pedestrian-friendly. There's much to see in the concentrated districts—especially cobblestoned Vieux-Montréal, where the city was born. Its architectural heritage has been substantially preserved, and restored 18th- and 19th-century structures now house shops, boutique hotels, galleries, cafes, bars, and apartments. Take this tour to get the lay of the land: You'll pass many of the neighborhood's highlights. START: **Métro: Place d'Armes.**

1 Banque de Montréal. This lavish neoclassical building was built in 1847. Though the exterior has remained largely unchanged, from 1901 to 1905 American architect Stanford White redid the interior, and in this enlarged space he created a vast lobby with high, green-marble columns. The public is welcome to stop in for a look. There's a free, tiny banking museum that illustrates the bank's early operations and displays a collection of 100-year-old mechanical banks. ⏱ *15 min. 129 rue St-Jacques.* ☎ *514/877-6810. Museum open Mon–Fri 10am–4pm.*

2 Place d'Armes. The architecture of the buildings that surround this outdoor plaza is representative of Montréal's growth: the Sulpician residence of the 17th century, the Banque de Montréal and Basilique Notre-Dame of the 19th century, and the Art Deco Edifice Aldred of the 20th century. (If the 23-story Aldred looks familiar, there's a reason: Built in 1931, it clearly resembles New York's Empire State Building, which was completed the same year.) The centerpiece of this square is a monument to city founder Paul de Chomedey, Sieur de Maisonneuve (1612–1676). These five statues mark the spot where settlers defeated Iroquois warriors in bloody hand-to-hand fighting, with de Maisonneuve himself locked in combat with the Iroquois chief. De Maisonneuve won and lived here another 23 years.

A ride through Vieux-Montréal in a horse-drawn carriage is a very popular activity for couples.

Note the dog depicted here—his bark alerted the settlers to the impending invasion. *Intersection of rues Notre-Dame and St-Sulpice.*

3 ★★★ Basilique Notre-Dame de Montréal. American architect James O'Donnell bucked the trend toward neoclassicism when he designed this Gothic Revival masterpiece. The exterior is somewhat reminiscent of the cathedral in Paris that it shares its name with, but this basilica's stunning interior sets it apart. The magnificent altar (carved from rare linden wood), the vaulted ceiling (studded with 24-karat gold stars), the 12-ton bell (among the largest in North America), and the

The Molson factory exterior is an easily identifiable landmark.

Limoges stained-glass windows (depicting moments from the city's history) are just some of the highlights. *See p 11, bullet* ⑥.

4P Claude Postel started out as a patisserie and chocolatier then added some tables and a short menu of daily hot specials. Customers come for paninis, pâtés, pastries, and made-to-order sandwiches. *75 rue Notre-Dame ouest.* ☎ *514/844-8750. www.claudepostel.com $.*

⑤ **Vieux Palais de Justice.** Court sessions ceased here for good in 1978 when the newer Palais de Justice was erected next door, but the Old Court House continues to serve the city as a civic office building. Though the building was completed in 1856, the dome and the top floor were added in 1891. Take a close look and you'll be able to spot the differences. A more modern landmark is also on display near here: Looking east on rue Notre-Dame, you should be able to see the Molson beer factory in the distance. *155 rue Notre-Dame est.*

⑥ ★ **Place Jacques-Cartier.** Opened in 1804 as a marketplace,

this central plaza is a magnet for locals and visitors year-round. In summer, performers fill the air with music, outdoor cafes serve as perches for people-watchers, and artists try to convince tourists to serve as their subjects. As you stroll past the 17th-century houses that line the promenade, observe the steeply pitched roofs, which were designed to shed heavy winter snows, and the small windows with double casements that let in light while keeping out wintry breezes. *Btw. rues Notre-Dame and de la Commune.*

⑦ **Hôtel de Ville (City Hall).** This ornate building has been Montréal's official City Hall since 1878, and it was here, in 1967, that French president Charles de Gaulle delighted Québec separatists by shouting from the balcony, "Vive le Québec libre!" (Long live free Québec!) *275 rue Notre-Dame est.*

⑧ **La Maison Pierre du Calvet.** Built in the 18th century and sumptuously restored between 1964 and 1966, this house was inhabited by a well-to-do family in its first years. Pierre du Calvet,

A statue of the Virgin Mary presides over the Chapelle Notre-Dame-de-Bon-Secours, also known as Sailors' Church.

believed to be the original owner, was a French Huguenot who supported the American Revolution and met here with Benjamin Franklin in 1775 (Calvet was later imprisoned for supplying money to the radicals south of the border). With a characteristic sloped roof and raised end walls that serve as firebreaks, the building is constructed of Montréal gray stone. It is now a hostellerie and restaurant. Visitors are invited to come in for a look. *See p 128.*

⑨ **Chapelle Notre-Dame-de-Bon-Secours.** It's only fitting that a city so reliant on its location near a river has a place of worship nicknamed the Sailors' Church. Many survivors from some of the sea's worst tragedies have made pilgrimages to this little chapel to give thanks for their good fortune (check out the ship models hanging from the chapel's ceiling). Marguerite-Bourgeoys, a pioneering nun, founded the church in this spot in 1675 (although the present building dates to 1773). She was beatified for her work by Pope Pius XII in 1950 and canonized and made a saint by Pope John Paul II in 1982. Set aside 15 minutes to browse the small museum, located in a crypt below the chapel. ⏱ *15 min. 400 rue St-Paul.* ☎ *514/282-8670. www. marguerite-bourgeoys.com. May–Oct Tues–Sun 10am–5:30pm; Nov to mid-Jan and Mar–Apr Tues–Sun 11am–3:30pm. Free admission to chapel. Museum C$8 adults, C$5 seniors and students, C$4 children 6–12, free for children 5 and under. Cash only. Métro: Champ-de-Mars.*

⑩ **Marché Bonsecours.** Like so many landmark buildings in Montréal, the Bonsecours market has been used for a variety of purposes. Completed in 1847, it first was home to the Parliament of United Canada, then served as Montréal's

The beautiful Basilique-Cathédrale Marie-Reine-du-Monde was built to resemble Rome's St. Peter's Basilica.

City Hall, and eventually housed the municipality's housing and planning offices. It was restored in 1992 for the city's 350th birthday celebration and now is a retail center with art shops, clothing boutiques, and sidewalk cafes. It's most renowned, however, for its massive dome, which served as a landmark for seafarers sailing into the harbor. Today it is lit at night. *350 rue St-Paul.* ☎ *514/872-7730. www.marche bonsecours.qc.ca. Open daily 10am–6pm (until 9pm during summer). Métro: Champ-de-Mars.*

For a good cafe to kick back in and just take in Vieux-Montréal, head to ⑪ **Jardin Nelson.** It has a porch adjacent to the plaza and a tree-shaded garden court where live jazz is presented every afternoon and evening. Pizzas and crepes dominate, with crepe options both sweet and savory (including lobster). When the weather's nice, it's open until 2am. It is closed November through mid-April. *407 Place Jacques-Cartier.* ☎ *514/861-5731. www.jardinnelson.com. $$.*

Downtown Montréal

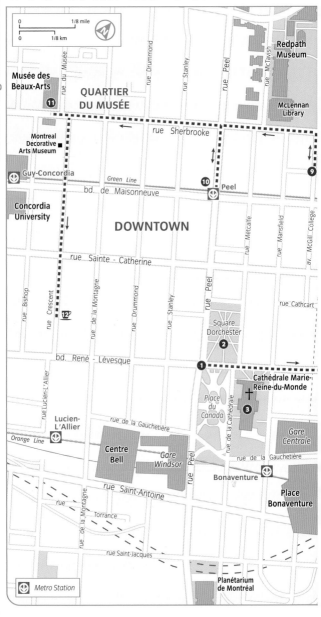

0 _____ 1/8 mile
0 _____ 1/8 km

Redpath Museum

rue du Musée

rue Drummond

rue Stanley

rue Peel

rue McTavish

Musée des Beaux-Arts
⑪

QUARTIER DU MUSÉE

McLennan Library

Montreal Decorative Arts Museum ■

rue Sherbrooke

Guy-Concordia

Green Line

⑩ Peel

⑨

Concordia University

bd. de Maisonneuve

DOWNTOWN

rue Metcalfe

rue Mansfield

av. McGill College

rue Sainte - Catherine

rue Bishop

rue Crescent

rue de la Montagne

rue Drummond

rue Stanley

rue Peel

⑫

rue Cathcart

Square Dorchester
②

bd. René - Lévesque

rue Lucien-L'Allier

Orange Line

Lucien-L'Allier

rue de la Gauchetière

①

Place du Canada

rue de la Cathédrale

Cathédrale Marie-Reine-du-Monde
✝
③

Gare Centrale

Centre Bell

Gare Windsor

rue Peel

rue de la Gauchetière

Bonaventure

Place Bonaventure

rue Saint-Antoine

rue de la Montagne

rue

Torrance

rue Saint-Jacques

🔲 **Metro Station**

Planétarium de Montréal

1 Boulevard René-Lévesque
2 Square Dorchester
3 Basilique-Cathédrale
   Marie-Reine-du-Monde
4 Place Ville-Marie
5 Rue Ste-Catherine
6 Cathédrale Christ Church
7 Java U
8 Rue Sherbrooke
9 *"The Illuminated Crowd"*
10 Café Vasco da Gama
11 Musée des Beaux-Arts
    (Museum of Fine Arts)
12 Brutopia

The core of downtown Montréal isn't as densely packed as those of other major cities in North America, but it's deceptively large. For that reason, it will probably take at least a half-day to make this tour into the city's commercial heart. START: **Métro: Bonaventure.**

❶ Boulevard René-Lévesque. Formerly Dorchester Boulevard, this primary street was renamed in 1988 following the death of René Lévesque, the Parti Québécois leader who led the movement for Québec independence and the use of the French language. Boulevard René-Lévesque is the city's broadest downtown thoroughfare. Start at the corner of boulevard René-Lévesque and rue Peel.

❷ Square Dorchester. This is one of downtown's central locations. It's a gathering point for tour buses and horse-drawn calèches, and the square's trees and benches invite lunchtime brown-baggers. This used to be called Dominion Square, but it was renamed for

Baron Dorchester, an early English governor, when the adjacent street, once named for Dorchester, was changed to boulevard René-Lévesque. Montréal's central tourist office is at the northern end of the park, at 1255 rue Peel, and is open daily. Visitors can ask questions of the bilingual attendants, purchase tour tickets, make hotel reservations, or arrange a car rental.

❸ Basilique-Cathédrale Marie-Reine-du-Monde. Suddenly get the feeling you're in Rome? This cathedral is a copy of St. Peter's Basilica in Vatican City, albeit roughly one-quarter of the size. It was built between 1875 and 1894 as the headquarters for Montréal's Roman Catholic bishop. The

Place Ville-Marie, designed by I. M. Pei is one of downtown's most important architectural landmarks.

statue in front is of Bishop Ignace Bourget (1799–1885), the force behind the construction. Most impressive is the 76m-high (249-ft.) dome, about a third of the size of the Rome original. The statues standing on the roofline represent patron saints of the Québec region, providing a local touch. *1085 rue de la Cathédrale.* ☎ *514/866-1661. www.cathedralecatholiquede montreal.org. Free admission, dona-tions welcome. Open Mon–Fri 7am–6:15pm; Sat–Sun 7:30am–6:15pm. Métro: Bonaventure.*

❹ **Place Ville-Marie.** One thing to keep in mind as you're touring Montréal is that the French word *place,* or *plaza,* sometimes means an outdoor square, as in Place Jacques-Cartier in Vieux-Montréal. Other times it refers to an indoor building or complex that includes stores and offices. Place Ville-Marie is in that second category. Known as PVM to Montréalers, the building is a glass box that was considered the gem of the 1960s urban redevel-opment efforts. Its architect was I. M. Pei, who also designed the glass pyramid at the Louvre in Paris. Pei gave the skyscraper a cross-shaped footprint, recalling the cross atop Mont-Royal. PVM is a great place to access the Underground City. *See p 91.*

❺ **Rue Ste-Catherine.** This is one of the city's prime shopping streets, and it pumps life into the surrounding areas day and night. It offers a 12-block stretch of stores that includes jeweler Henry Birks, Tommy Hilfiger, SAQ Signature, Kiehl's, Simons, Mango, Roots, H&M, Ogilvy, Apple, and Steve Madden—to name a sampling. Note that Ste-Catherine also has a smattering of adult strip clubs right alongside the family-friendly fare (there's a gigan-tic neon sign announcing Club

Rue Ste-Catherine is one of the city's prime thoroughfares for shopping.

Super Sexe, for instance). The mixed use of the street is a Mon-tréal signature.

❻ **Cathédrale Christ Church.** Built from 1856 to 1859, this neo-Gothic building is the seat of the Anglican bishop of Montréal. Its gar-den is modeled on a medieval Euro-pean cloister. In addition to Sunday's 10am Choral Eucharist and 4pm Choral Evensong, the church has services at noon and 5:15pm on weekdays. *See p 15, bullet* ❺.

At the corner of rues Union and Sherbrooke, you'll find an outpost of the jovial ❼ **Java U,** a local food chain that got its start in 1996 at Concordia University. In a high-design venue with friendly, laid-back staff, it serves quiches, salads, wraps, and cake. Also featured is ice cream from local purveyor Bilbo-quet. *626 rue Sherbrooke.* ☎ *514/ 286-1991. www.java-u.com. $.*

Picturesque McGill University is one of the most prestigious institutions of learning in Canada.

⑧ Rue Sherbrooke. This is the city's grand boulevard, still rich with former mansions, ritzy hotels, high-end boutiques, and special museums that give it its personality. The main campus of Canada's most prestigious school, McGill University, is here, along with the school's eclectic Musée McCord. The university was founded after a bequest from a Scottish-born fur trader, James McGill. The central campus mixes modern concrete and glass structures alongside older stone buildings and is the focal point for the school's 34,000 students. The McCord museum of Canadian history opened in 1921 and maintains an often eccentric collection of photographs, paintings, and First Nations folk art. Its special exhibits make it especially worth a visit. *See p 13, bullet ①.*

⑨ The Illuminated Crowd. This is an eggnog-colored work in polyester resin (1985) by sculptor Raymond Mason. The piece captures the faces of a life-size crowd of figures in a slew of emotional states: illumination, hope, hilarity, irritation, fear, violence, and "the flow of man's emotion through space" as it says on the descriptive plaque. The work is outdoors at the base of the all-glass BNP office tower near the intersection of avenue McGill College and avenue du President Kennedy. Mason was born in England but moved to Paris early in his career—giving his own life the mixture of British and French influences that is emblematic of Montréal. *1981 av. McGill College.*

Downtown is full of restaurants both fancy and casual, and right in between is **⑩ Café Vasco Da Gama,** a sleek, high-ceilinged eatery with a Portuguese feel—the

The Illuminated Crowd, a sculpture set just in front of the Banque National de Paris tower in downtown Montréal.

owners also run the esteemed Ferreira Café (p 100) on the same block. It's a great place for big breakfasts, pastries, sandwiches, burgers, and tapas. *1472 rue Peel.* ☎ *514/286-2688. www.vasco dagama.ca. $.*

⓫ Musée des Beaux-Arts de Montréal (Museum of Fine Arts). This is Montréal's most prominent museum. The modern annex on the south side of rue Sherbrooke was added in 1991 and is connected to the original stately Beaux-Arts building (1912) on the north side by an underground tunnel that doubles as a gallery. Special exhibitions have recently included Imagine: The Peace Ballad of John and Yoko and a dazzling collection of fashion creations by Yves Saint Laurent. *See p 13, bullet ❷.*

The original building of the Musée des Beaux-Arts de Montréal is home to its collection of decorative and Canadian art, among other works.

Lively spots for food and drink are abundant along rue Crescent. Thursday's and Sir Winston Churchill, at nos. 1449 and 1459, both have large, festive balconies that overlook the street.

⓬ Brutopia, at no. 1219, pulls endless pints of a half dozen of its own microbrews which are made right on-site. With several rooms on three levels, a terrace in back, and its own street-side balcony, Brutopia draws students with laptops and old friends just hanging out. The snacking menu spans the globe. Bands perform, too, with an open-mic night on Sunday. *See p 110.*

Colorful circular art on the walls of the Peel Métro station.

Plateau Mont-Royal

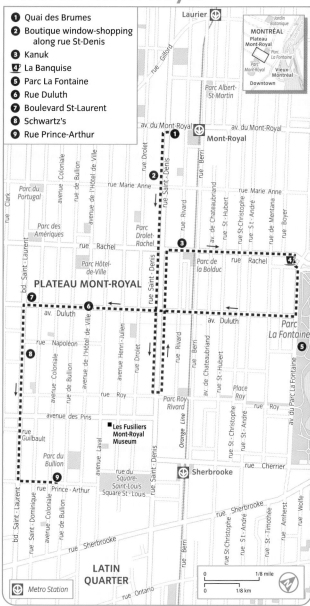

1. Quai des Brumes
2. Boutique window-shopping along rue St-Denis
3. Kanuk
4. La Banquise
5. Parc La Fontaine
6. Rue Duluth
7. Boulevard St-Laurent
8. Schwartz's
9. Rue Prince-Arthur

MONTRÉAL

Jardin Botanique

Plateau Mont-Royal

Parc La Fontaine

Parc Mont-Royal

Vieux-Montréal

Downtown

Laurier

rue Gilford

Parc Albert-St-Martin

av. du Mont-Royal

Mont-Royal

rue Drolet

rue Berri

rue Saint-Denis

av. du Mont-Royal

Parc du Portugal

avenue Colaniale

rue de Bullion

avenue de l'Hôtel-de-Ville

rue Marie-Anne

rue Rivard

av. de Chateaubriand

rue Marie-Anne

rue St-Hubert

rue St-Christophe

rue St-André

rue de Mentana

rue Boyer

rue Clark

Parc des Amériques

rue Rachel

Parc Drolet-Rachel

Parc Hôtel-de-Ville

PLATEAU MONT-ROYAL

Parc de la Bolduc

rue Rachel

bd. Saint-Laurent

rue Saint-Denis

av. Duluth

av. Duluth

Parc La Fontaine

rue Napoléon

avenue de l'Hôtel-de-Ville

avenue Henri-Julien

rue Drolet

rue Rivard

rue Berri

av. de Chateaubriand

rue St-Hubert

av. du Parc La Fontaine

avenue Colaniale

rue de Bullion

rue Roy

Parc Roy Rivard

Place Roy

rue Roy

avenue des Pins

Les Fusiliers Mont-Royal Museum

Orange Line

rue St-Christophe

rue St-André

rue Guilbault

avenue Laval

rue Saint-Denis

rue Cherrier

Parc du Bullion

rue Prince-Arthur

rue du Square-Saint-Louis Square St-Louis

Sherbrooke

bd. Saint-Laurent

rue Saint-Dominique

avenue Colaniale

avenue de Bullion

rue Sherbrooke

rue Berri

rue St-Christophe

rue St-André

rue St-Timothée

rue Amherst

rue Wolfe

LATIN QUARTER

rue Sherbrooke

rue Ontario

Metro Station

| 0 | | 1/8 mile |
| 0 | | 1/8 km |

This is essentially a browsing and grazing tour, designed to provide a sampling of the sea of ethnicities that make up Plateau Mont-Royal. The largely Francophone (French-speaking) neighborhood has seen an unprecedented flourishing of restaurants, cafes, clubs, and shops in recent years, and the residential side streets are filled with row houses that are home to students, young professionals, and immigrants old and new. It's bounded more or less by rue Sherbrooke on the south, boulevard St-Joseph on the north, boulevard St-Laurent on the west, and avenue Papineau on the east.

START: **Métro: Mont-Royal.**

❶ Quai des Brumes. Electronic, rock, jazz, and blues music—this popular gathering spot offers live music most evenings, and drinking during the day. *4481 rue St-Denis.* ☎ *514/499-0467. www.myspace. com/quaidesbrumes.*

❷ Boutique window-shopping along St-Denis. From avenue du Mont-Royal in the north to rue Roy (and farther) to the south, this main drag is thick with great places to poke around. Renaud-Bray, at no. 4380, is a large bookstore with mostly French stock as well as CDs, magazines, and newspapers from around the world. Jacob, at no. 4268, and Bedo, at no. 4228, are Canadian clothing chains for the young and the fun. Zone, at no. 4246, is part of a small Montréal-based chain that specializes in contemporary housewares, sleekly monochromatic and brightly hued. Kaliyana, at 4107, is another Canadian clothing company, offering natural-fiber outfits that are flowing and angular—think Asian-influenced Eileen Fisher. (A reminder: Only cross streets at the corners; jaywalking is illegal and police regularly hand out tickets.)

❸ Kanuk. One of Canada's top manufacturers of high-end winter coats and accessories designs, sews, and sells its wares right here. Like EMS or L.L.Bean in the U.S., Kanuk first sold its heavy parkas primarily to

Many charming boutiques are located in Plateau Mont-Royal.

outdoor enthusiasts. Back then, the company wryly notes on its website, customers had a choice of royal blue or royal blue. Today, its jackets come in 36 colors and 70 models. The showroom's fluorescent lighting and mile-high racks of coats does not suggest luxury, although a parka can set you back C$600 to C$900. They're an extremely popular practical necessity—and a status symbol. *See p 87.*

Kanuk is a Montréal institution.

If you haven't yet tried poutine, the national comfort food, by all means hop into **4** **La Banquise.** The restaurant is practically a city landmark with its 25 variations of the french fries with cheese curds. The funky little restaurant is open 24 hours a day, every day. *See p 100.*

5 **Parc La Fontaine.** Strolling this grand park, particularly on a warm day, is an enormously satisfying way to see Montréal at play. This northwestern end of La Fontaine is well used by people and puppies of all ages. There's a bike-rental shop (www.cyclepop.ca) before you enter the park at 1000 rue Rachel est if you're keen to pedal around. *See p 20, bullet* **6**.

6 **Rue Duluth.** This somewhat drab street is dotted with an ever-changing collection of Greek, Portuguese, Italian, North African, Malaysian, and Vietnamese eateries. Many of the restaurants state that you can *apportez votre vin* (bring your own wine). There are also several small antiques shops here. *Rue Duluth btw. the parc and bd. St-Laurent.*

7 **Boulevard St-Laurent.** St-Laurent is the north-south thoroughfare that divides Montréal into its east and west sides. It's so prominent in Montréal's cultural history that it's known to Anglophones (English speakers), Francophones (French speakers), and Allophones (people whose primary language is neither English nor French) simply as "the Main." Traditionally a beachhead for immigrants to the city, St-Laurent has become a street of bistros and clubs. The late-night section runs for several miles, roughly from rue Laurier in the north down to rue Sherbrooke in the south. The boom in entertainment venues was fueled by low rent prices and the large number of industrial lofts in this area, a legacy of St-Laurent's heyday as a garment-manufacturing center. Today, these cavernous spaces are places for the city's hipsters, professionals, artists, and guests to eat and play. Many spots have the life span of a firefly, but some pound on for years.

8 **Schwartz's.** The language police insisted on the exterior sign with the French mouthful (SCHWARZ CHARCUTERIE HEBRAIQUE DE MONTRÉAL), but everyone just calls it Schwartz's. This narrow, no-frills Hebrew deli might appear completely unassuming, but it serves the smoked meat against which all other smoked meats are measured. *See p 103.*

9 **Rue Prince-Arthur.** Named after Queen Victoria's third son, who was governor-general of Canada from 1911 to 1916, this pedestrian street is filled with bars and

Jewish Montréal

At the turn of the 20th century, Montréal was home to more Jews than any other Canadian city, attracting an especially large Yiddish-speaking population from Eastern Europe. Today Toronto has nearly twice as many Jewish residents, but vestiges of the community's history and ongoing practices remain here.

The Bagg Street Shul, at the corner of rue Clark (1 block west of bd. St-Laurent) and rue Bagg (1 block south of rue Duluth), began as a two-family residence and was converted to a synagogue in 1920 and 1921. It has been in continuous use ever since. Other synagogues dot the neighborhood but have transitioned as the Jewish community dispersed—one became a French college, another an evangelical church (though it still houses 10 murals of the history of Jews in Montréal).

Kosher edibles abound. One could start the day with a bagel from either **St-Viateur Bagel & Café** (1127 av. Mont-Royal est), or **Fairmont Bagel** (74 av. Fairmont ouest), a few blocks farther north, and then travel back in time for lunch with an old-school fountain soda from **Wilensky Light Lunch** (34 rue Fairmount ouest). For dinner, there's always **Schwartz's** (earlier) or steaks at the posh **Moishes** (3961 bd. St-Laurent).

The Snowden neighborhood in western Montréal is home to the city's contemporary Jewish organizations. The **Jewish Public Library** (☎ 514/345-2627; www.jewishpubliclibrary.org) boasts the largest circulating collection of Judaica in North America and hosts lectures, cultural events, and concerts. Its archive of more than 17,000 photos of Montréal's Jewish history is in the process of being digitized to be put online. The library shares a building at 5151 Côte-Ste-Catherine with the **Montréal Holocaust Memorial Centre** (☎ 514/345-2605; www.mhmc.ca) and two dozen other Jewish community service agencies. The memorial center features exhibits to commemorate lives lost in the Holocaust. Just across the street is the **Segal Centre for Performing Arts** (p 122), which presents plays in Yiddish.

restaurants which add more to the area's liveliness than to the city's gastronomic reputation. The older establishments go by such names as La Cabane Grecque, La Caverne Grec, Casa Grecque—no doubt you will discern an emerging theme—but the Greek stalwarts are being challenged by Latino and Asian newcomers. Their owners vie constantly with gimmicks to haul in passersby, including two-for-one drinks and dueling *tables d'hôte*. Tables and chairs are set out along the sides of the street, and in warm weather, street performers, vendors, and caricaturists also compete for tourist dollars.

Parc du Mont-Royal

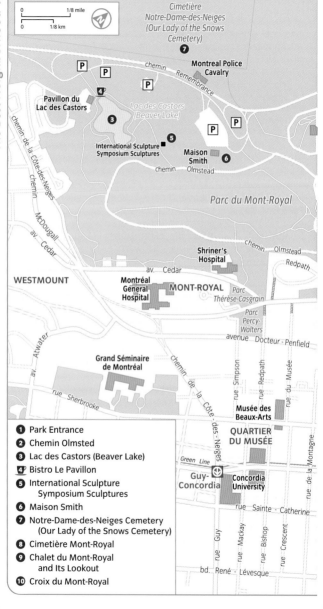

1 Park Entrance
2 Chemin Olmsted
3 Lac des Castors (Beaver Lake)
4 Bistro Le Pavillon
5 International Sculpture
   Symposium Sculptures
6 Maison Smith
7 Notre-Dame-des-Neiges Cemetery
   (Our Lady of the Snows Cemetery)
8 Cimetière Mont-Royal
9 Chalet du Mont-Royal
   and Its Lookout
10 Croix du Mont-Royal

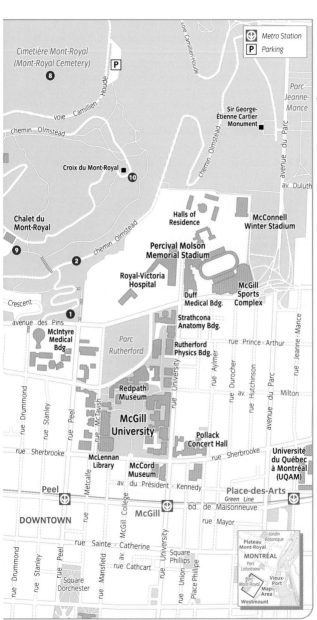

Metro Station
P Parking

Cimetière Mont-Royal
(Mont-Royal Cemetery)
8

P

voie Camillien - Houde

chemin Olmstead

Sir George-
Étienne Cartier
Monument ■

Parc
Jeanne-
Mance

avenue du Parc

av. Duluth

Croix du Mont-Royal ■
10

Chalet du
Mont-Royal

9

2

chemin Olmstead

Halls of
Residence

McConnell
Winter Stadium

**Percival Molson
Memorial Stadium**

Crescent

1

avenue des Pins

**Royal-Victoria
Hospital**

Duff
Medical Bdg.

McGill
Sports
Complex

**McIntyre
Medical
Bdg.**

Parc
Rutherford

Strathcona
Anatomy Bdg.

rue Prince - Arthur

Rutherford
Physics Bdg.

rue Aylmer

rue Durocher

rue Hutchinson

Milton

avenue du Parc

rue Jeanne - Mance

rue Drummond

rue Stanley

rue Peel

rue McTavish

rue University

**Redpath
Museum**

**McGill
University**

**Pollack
Concert Hall**

rue Sherbrooke

rue Sherbrooke

**Université
du Québec
à Montréal
(UQAM)**

**McLennan
Library**

**McCord
Museum**

av. du Président - Kennedy

Place-des-Arts
Green Line

Peel

Metcalfe

rue McGill - College

McGill

bd. de Maisonneuve

DOWNTOWN

rue Peel

rue University

rue Mayor

rue Drummond

rue Stanley

rue Peel

rue Mansfield

av. McGill - College

rue Sainte - Catherine

av. University

rue Cathcart

Square
Phillips

rue Union

Place Phillip

Square
Dorchester

Plateau
Mont-Royal

*Jardin
Botanique*

MONTRÉAL

Parc
Lafontaine

Parc
Mont-Royal
Map
Area

Vieux-
Port

Westmount

Montréal's largest green space may also be the most tax-ing on a sightseer's legs, given the park's occasionally steep hills and staircases. That said, there are options for staying on a broad, lightly graded bridle path, so you need only be in reasonably good shape to tackle the 200-hectare (494-acre) park. The small mountain for which Montréal is named is a popular place for walkers, runners, and anyone seeking out broad panoramas of the city. If you're carrying a PDA or a phone with Internet access, you can pull up a terrific interactive map at www.lemontroyal.qc.ca/carte/en/index.sn. You can also download podcasts for guided audio-video walks from the same website. START: **Corner of rue Peel and avenue des Pins.**

❶ Park Entrance. There are limited entry points to the park, and this is the most direct from downtown. Note that this entrance has been under construction, but you can still wend your way in. It's possible to reach the top of this small mountain by several routes from this spot. Those looking for a workout (and the shortest, fastest route) will want to take the steepest set of stairs at every opportunity. Those who want to take their time and make the climb more gradually should stay on the switchback bridle path, originally designed for horse-drawn carriages. *Corner of rue Peel and av. des Pins.*

Montréalers of all ages enjoy Parc du Mont-Royal's lovely greenery.

❷ ★ Chemin Olmsted. The broad path that loops through the park was named for the park's designer, American landscape architect Frederick Law Olmsted (1802–1903), who also designed Central Park in New York City. It's actually the only part of Olmstead's design that became a reality as the rest of the park wasn't completed to his scheme. Walkers, joggers, mountain bikers, and mounted policemen all cross paths here. The road is closed to vehicular traffic, making it a joy for those looking for peace and quiet from the city.

❸ ★ Lac des Castors (Beaver Lake). During the summer, sun-bathers and picnickers cover the grassy swaths surrounding Beaver Lake, which itself is filled with people in paddle boats. When the mercury drops and snow falls, they're all replaced by Montréalers on ice skates—an artificial rink is set up adjacent to the lake every winter (the lake itself isn't stable enough to support skaters when frozen). The nearby pavilion rents skates and features a bronzed pair near the entrance that belonged to Jean Beliveau, a revered hockey player for the Montréal Canadiens. He wore this very pair of CCM Tackaberry skates when he notched his 500th goal in 1971.

4 Bistro Le Pavillon is a French restaurant that looks out on Beaver Lake. Run by the Holder brothers, who also run the popular Holder restaurant in Vieux-Montréal, it features lobster bisque, duck confit salad, and steak. It's open daily until 10pm in summer and Wednesday through Sunday the rest of the year. There's also a more modest cafeteria on-site and an area for picnicking. *2000 chemin Remembrance.* ☎ *514/849-2002.*

One of the International Sculpture Symposium works in Parc Mont-Royal.

5 International Sculpture Symposium sculptures. On the grassy rise to the east of Beaver Lake sit several stone and metal structures. These sculptures were erected in 1964 as part of the International Sculpture Symposium in Montréal. A collection of artists was given marble, granite, or metal to shape their abstract visions, and a limited amount of time to complete their work. The representation of four priestesses, made in Italian marble by Yerassimos Sklavos (1927–1967), is one of the most striking pieces. Not far from the sculptures, see if you can find two granite plaques (out of a total of five such plaques spread around the park) that have poetic phrases or humorous quips by Montréaler Gilbert Boyer chiseled into the rock. *Near Beaver Lake.*

6 ★ Maison Smith. The park's year-round information center has restrooms, a gift shop, and a set of educational displays that describe the history, flora, and fauna of Mont-Royal. Café Smith, a terrace restaurant, offers soups, sandwiches, beverages, and sweets. There's a parking lot here if you choose to drive to the park instead of walk. *1260 chemin Remembrance. www. lemontroyal.qc.ca.*

7 Notre-Dame-des-Neiges Cemetery (Our Lady of the Snows Cemetery). Many famous Montréalers have been laid to rest in the city's largest, and mostly Catholic, cemetery. Included are the Molson crypts, where members of the influential Canadian brewing family are buried. Other prominent residents include statesman Sir George-Etienne Cartier, poet Emile Nelligan, architect Ernest Cormier, and hockey star Maurice "The Rocket" Richard. The cemetery's website offers a search function to locate specific graves. *4601 chemin Côte-des-Neiges.* ☎ *514/735-1361. www.cimetierenddn.org.*

8 Cimetière Mont-Royal. Smaller than its Catholic neighbor to the west, Mont Royal Cemetery was founded in 1852 by a group of Christian (but non-Catholic) denominations. The beautifully terraced cemetery was designed to resemble a garden and makes for peaceful

Statue of Sir George-Etienne Cartier.

View from the lookout of the Chalet du Mont-Royal.

strolling. Among those interred here is Anna Leonowens, the British governess who was the real-life inspiration for the musical comedy *The King and I*. **1297 chemin de la Fôret.** ☎ **514/279-7358. www. mountroyalcem.com.**

⑨ ★ Chalet du Mont-Royal and its lookout. The front terrace here offers the most popular panoramic view of the city and the river. A few telescopes are available so you can make a more detailed

study of the skyscrapers and St. Lawrence. The chalet itself was constructed from 1931 to 1932 and has been used over the years for receptions and concerts. Inside, take a look at the 17 paintings hanging just below the ceiling, starting to the right of the door. They relate the region's history and the story of the French explorations of North America.

⑩ Croix du Mont-Royal. Legend has it that Montréal founder de Maisonneuve erected a wooden cross here in 1643 after the young colony survived a flood threat. The present incarnation is a steel cross that was installed in 1924. It's lit at night and is visible from all over the city. Beside the cross is a plaque marking where a time capsule was interred in August 1992, during Montréal's 350th-birthday celebration. Some 12,000 children ages 6 to 12 filled the capsule with messages and drawings depicting their visions for the city in the year 2142, when Montréal will be 500 years old and the capsule will be opened. ●

Montréal's famous Steel Cross sits atop Mont-Royal.

Extreme Weather in Montréal

For the most part, Montréal lives in either winter or summer—the spring and fall seasons are sweet but short-lived. Winter lasts from November until late March, and summer lasts from June through September. The cold months often include snow blizzards, freezing rain, and ice storms (in Jan 1998, one of the worst ice storms in history crippled the city by destroying power lines and sending citizens to their fireplaces for warmth). Summers often include stifling humidity during July and August. Luckily, there's an Underground City below much of downtown, with miles of shops, restaurants, movie theaters, and connections to the subway (see p 91 for a brief tour).

The Best **Shopping**

Montréal **Shopping**

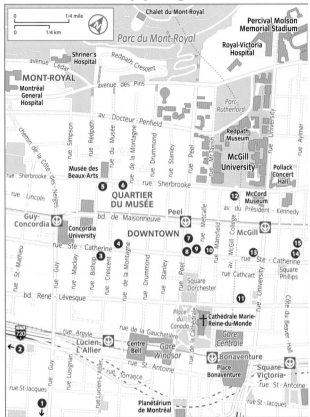

Previous page: The locally produced Domaine Pinnacle ice apple wine is quite popular, and has won numerous awards.

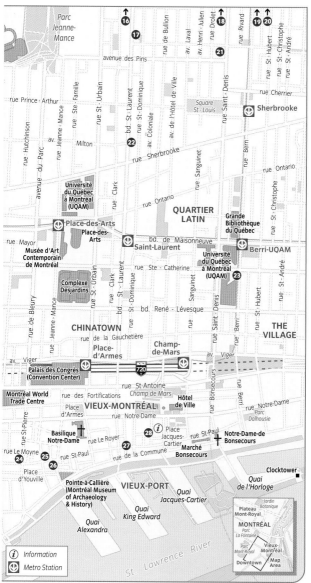

Parc
Jeanne-
Mance

16
17
rue de Bullion
rue Laval
av. Henri-Julien
rue Drolet
18
rue Rivard
19 **20**
rue St-Hubert
rue St-Christophe
rue St-André

avenue des Pins

21

rue Prince-Arthur

rue Hutchinson
av. du Parc
rue Jeanne-Mance
rue Ste-Famille
rue St-Urbain
bd. St-Laurent
rue St-Dominique
av. Coloniale
av. de l'Hôtel de Ville

rue Saint-Denis
Square
St-Louis

rue Cherrier

🔽 **Sherbrooke**

Milton

22

rue Sherbrooke

rue Clark

rue Berri
rue St-Christophe

Université
du Québec
à Montréal
(UQAM)

rue Ontario

rue Ontario

rue Sanguinet

**QUARTIER
LATIN**

Grande
Bibliothèque
du Québec

🔽 **Place-des-Arts**
Place-des-Arts

🔽 **Saint-Laurent**
bd. de Maisonneuve

🔽 **Berri-UQAM**

rue Mayor

Musée d'Art
Contemporain
de Montréal

rue Ste-Catherine

Université
du Québec
à Montréal
(UQAM)
23

rue St-Hubert

Complexe
Desjardins

rue St-Urbain
rue Clark
bd. St-Laurent
rue St-Dominique
rue Sanguinet
rue Saint-Denis
rue Berri
rue St-André

bd. René-Lévesque

rue de Bleury
rue Jeanne-Mance

CHINATOWN
rue de la Gauchetière

**Champ-
de-Mars**

**THE
VILLAGE**

🔽 **Place-
d'Armes**

🔽 **Champ-
de-Mars**

av. Viger

av. Viger

rue Bonsecours
rue Berri

**Palais des Congrès
(Convention Center)**
720

**Montréal World
Trade Centre**

rue des Fortifications
Champ de Mars

rue St-Antoine

Place
d'Armes

VIEUX-MONTRÉAL
rue Notre-Dame

**Hôtel
de Ville**

rue Notre-Dame
Parc
Dalhousie

rue St-Pierre
**Basilique
Notre-Dame**
✝
rue Le Royer

28 ⓘ Place
Jacques-
Cartier

rue St-Paul

**Notre-Dame-de-
Bonsecours** ✝

rue Le Moyne
25
24
26
rue St-Paul
rue de la Commune

27

**Marché
Bonsecours**

**Pointe-à-Callière
(Montréal Museum
of Archaeology
& History)**

Place
d'Youville

VIEUX-PORT
*Quai
Jacques-Cartier*

Clocktower ▪

*Quai
de l'Horloge*

*Quai
King Edward*

*Quai
Alexandra*

*Jardin
Botanique*

Plateau
Mont-Royal

MONTRÉAL
Parc
La Fontaine

Parc
Mont-Royal

Vieux-
Montréal

Map
Area

Downtown

St. Lawrence River

ⓘ Information
🔽 Metro Station

Shopping Best Bets

Best **Department Store for High Fashion**
Holt Renfrew, *1300 rue Sherbrooke ouest (p 86)*

Best **Department Store for Teen Fashion**
Simons, *977 rue Ste-Catherine ouest (p 86)*

Best **Store for Warding-Off-Winter Fashion**
Kanuk, *485 rue Rachel est (p 87)*

Best **Antiques**
Antique Alley, *rue Notre-Dame ouest (p 85)*

Best **Edgy Art Gallery**
Yves Laroche Galerie d'Art, *4 rue St-Paul est (p 85)*

Best **Goofy Gift Store**
Mortimer Snodgrass, *209 rue St-Paul ouest (p 89)*

Best **Shop for Tracking Down Rare Records**
Beatnick's, *3770 rue St-Denis (p 90)*

La Baie, Canada's oldest retailer, has been in business for more than 115 years.

Best **Food Market**
Marché Atwater, *138 rue Atwater (p 88)*

Best **Gourmet Food**
La Vieille Europe, *3855 bd. St-Laurent (p 88)*

Best **Chocolate Shop**
Les Chocolats de Chloé, *546 rue Duluth est;* and Suite 88 Chocolatier, *3957 rue St-Denis (p 88)*

Best **Wine Shop**
SAQ Signature, *677 rue Ste-Catherine ouest (p 89)*

Best **Locally Made Bags Using Recycled Billboards**
Galerie Zone Orange *410 rue St-Pierre (p 85)*

Best **High-End Inuit Sculpture**
Galerie Le Chariot, *446 Place Jacques-Cartier (p 85)*

Best **Wool Blanket**
La Baie (The Bay), *585 Ste-Catherine ouest (p 86)*

Best **Store for Seeing a Bagpiper**
Ogilvy, *1307 Ste-Catherine ouest (p 86)*

Best **Snazzy Housewares**
Arthur Quentin, *3960 rue St-Denis (p 89)*

Best **Museum Shop**
Musée des Beaux-Arts Boutique, *1390 rue Sherbrooke ouest (p 90)*

Best **Mall to Start Exploring the Underground City**
Place Ville-Marie, *4 Place Ville Marie (p 91)*

Best **Avant-Garde Clothing for Women**
Kaliyana, *4107 rue St-Denis (p 87)*

Montréal Shopping **A to Z**

Antiques, Arts & Crafts & Galleries

★★ **Antique Alley** VIEUX-MON-TREAL   Some of the city's quirkier antiques shops have disappeared in recent years—thanks a lot, eBay. But there are still tempting shops along Antique Alley, as it's nicknamed, a strip of rue Notre-Dame west of Vieux-Montréal. *Rue Notre-Dame ouest, especially btw. rue Guy and av. Atwater. Métro: Lionel-Groulx.*

★ **Galerie Le Chariot** VIEUX-MON-TREAL   Galleries that feature Inuit art are peppered throughout the city, and Le Chariot's showroom is among the most central, directly on Place Jacques-Cartier in the heart of Vieux-Montréal. Here shoppers can find handmade pieces by Inuk artists from Cape Dorset, Lake Harbour, and Baffin Island—carved bears, seals, owls, and tableaus of mothers and children. Pieces range in price from C$150 to C$25,000 and are certified by the Canadian government. *446 Place Jacques-Cartier.* ☎ *514/875-4994. www.galerielechariot.com. AE, MC, V. Métro: Place d'Armes.*

Galerie Zone Orange VIEUX-MONTREAL   Angry sock monkeys, wildly creative jewelry, and colorful ceramics from 30 regional artists are on display at the small Zone Orange, which also has a tiny espresso bar in its center. Perhaps the coolest products are the light-weight bags made from recycled billboards and streetlamp banners by the ecofocused Atelier Entre-Peaux (www.entre-peaux-ecode sign.com), a Montréal company; its bike bags run about C$69. *410 rue St-Pierre.* ☎ *514/510-5809. AE, MC, V. Métro: Place d'Armes.*

★ **Yves Laroche Galerie d'Art** VIEUX-MONTREAL   High art meets punk rock. The large paintings and prints on display here include works by Shepard Fairey, the American artist who designed both the Obama graphic that became the signature image of the 2008 U.S. presidential campaign and the ubiquitous OBEY stickers, which are postered illegally all over the U.S. The store sells graphic novels and collectible figurines as well. Its blog-style website is engaging. *4 rue St-Paul est.* ☎ *514/393-1999. www.yveslaroche.com. AE, MC, V. Métro: Place d'Armes.*

Books

Paragraphe DOWNTOWN   Though it caters to university students seeking course materials, this store's many shelves are also stocked with a decent selection of novels and classics. Once in a while the shop's couches are cleared out for in-store author appearances and small-scale musical performances. *2220 av. McGill College.* ☎ *514/845-5811. www.paragraphbooks.com. AE, MC, V. Métro: McGill.*

kids Renaud-Bray PLATEAU MONT-ROYAL   For those who know French or want to brush up, this two-level bookstore with a primarily French-language stock is a valuable resource. It also sells tapes, DVDs, CDs, and newspapers and magazines from all over the world. Most English-language books are on the upper floor. There's a large children's section, too. *4380 rue St-Denis.* ☎ *514/844-2587. www.renaud-bray.com. AE, MC, V. Métro: Mont-Royal.*

Montréal's Underground City

Montréal's harsh winters and sticky summers were the motivating force behind the construction of a series of underground tunnels that has created a network of subterranean shops, cafes, and entrances to hotels and Métro stations. This monumental achievement in urban planning stretches for nearly 33km (21 miles) and typically sees 500,000 people passing through each day. You can buy a new outfit, take in some art, or even catch a movie—all without ever venturing outdoors. To head *souterrain* from street level, look for blue signs with a white arrow pointing down or signs marked "RESO." You can also enter at the many malls which operate both above and below ground. For more information see "Exploring the Underground City," later in this chapter.

Department Stores

Also see "Exploring the Underground City," later in this chapter, for some of the city's larger shopping complexes.

★ kids Holt Renfrew DOWNTOWN   After starting life as a furrier in 1837, Holt Renfrew has evolved into a store for clothes shoppers with big budgets and big taste. Hermès, Armani, Stuart Weitzman, and Stella McCartney are just a few of the designer labels you'll find. *1300 rue Sherbrooke ouest.* ☎ *514/842-5111. AE, DC, MC, V. Métro: Peel.*

★ La Baie (The Bay) DOWNTOWN   No retailer has an older or more celebrated pedigree than the Hudson's Bay Company, whose name was shortened to "The Bay" and then transformed into "La Baie" by Québec language laws. The company was incorporated in Canada in 1670. Its main store focuses on clothing but also offers crystal, china, Inuit carvings, and its famous Hudson's Bay "point blanket." The company is the official outfitter of the Canadian Olympic teams in 2010 and 2012. *585 Ste-Catherine ouest.* ☎ *514/281-4422. www.hbc.com. AE, MC, V. Métro: McGill.*

★★ Ogilvy DOWNTOWN   This most vibrant example of a classy breed of department store that appears to be fading from the scene was established in 1866 and has been at this location since 1912. A bagpiper still announces the noon hour (a favorite sight for tourists). Special events, glowing chandeliers, and wide aisles also enhance the shopping experience. Ogilvy has always had a reputation for quality merchandise and now contains more than 60 boutiques, including Louis Vuitton, Anne Klein, and Burberry. Its Christmas windows are eagerly awaited each season. *1307 rue Ste-Catherine ouest.* ☎ *514/842-7711. www.ogilvycanada.com. AE, MC, V. Métro: Peel.*

kids Simons DOWNTOWN   This branch was the first expansion for Québec City's long-established family-owned department store. A must for teen shoppers, Simons takes the labels-within-a-store approach now popular at trendy but affordable chains such as H&M or Forever 21, and throws in a few cutting-edge designers for inspiration. *977 rue Ste-Catherine ouest.* ☎ *514/282-1840. AE, MC, V. Métro: Peel.*

Fashion

Montréal Fashion Week happens every March. The 2009 event took place at the Marché Bonsecours and featured 20 Canadian designers including Harricana (below). Photos and links are online at www.montreal fashionweek.ca. The Montréal Fashion & Design Festival happens on avenue de McGill College each June; see www.festivalmodedesign.com.

Club Monaco DOWNTOWN   A trendier version of Banana Republic, and cheaper than Prada, this Canadian-gone-global chain has a refined edge, using simple, bold colors in clothes for both sexes. *Les Cours Mont Royal, 1455 rue Peel, Ste. 226.* ☎ 514/499-0959. *www.clubmonaco. com. AE, MC, V. Métro: Peel.*

kids Crocs DOWNTOWN   Fun fact: The marshmallowy, brightly colored foam clog originated in Québec—who knew? It was acquired by the American Crocs company in 2004 and these days the shoes are likely to be manufactured in Mexico or China. The company has branched into more normal-looking (read: less childlike) footwear, and opened a store in the heart of downtown in 2008. *1382 rue Ste-Catherine ouest.* ☎ 514/750-9796. *AE, MC, V. Métro: Guy-Concordia.*

Fourrures Dubarry Furs VIEUX-MONTRÉAL   A nod back to the city's history in fur trading. Coats and capes in fur, shearling, cashmere, and leather, along with hats, earmuffs, purses, and scarves, are all on display at the family-run, high-end Dubarry Furs. *206 rue St-Paul ouest.* ☎ 514/844-7483. *www.dubarryfurs. com. AE, DC, MC, V. Métro: Place d'Armes.*

Harricana DOWNTOWN   Designer Mariouche Gagné takes her unique cue from the city's long history with the fur trade, recycling old fur into funky patchwork garments. A leader in the so-called ecoluxe movement, Gagné also recycles silk scarves, turning them into tops and skirts. Her boutique is close to the Marché Atwater (p 88). *3000 rue St-Antoine ouest.* ☎ 877/894-9919 or 514/287-6517. *www.harricana.qc.ca. AE, MC, V. Métro: Lionel-Groulx.*

★ **Harry Rosen** DOWNTOWN   For more than 50 years, this well-known retailer of designer suits and accessories has been making men look good in Armani, Dolce & Gabbana, and its own Harry Rosen Made in Italy line. The store's website features a nifty timeline of the shop's evolution from a Toronto made-to-measure store to a national leader in men's fashion. *1455 rue Peel.* ☎ 514/284-3315. *www.harry rosen.com. AE, MC, V. Métro: Peel.*

★ **Kaliyana** PLATEAU   Vaguely Japanese and certainly minimalist, the free-flowing garments sold here are largely asymmetrical separates. Made by a Canadian designer, they come in muted tones of solid colors. Ask for "the kit" (C\$995) and you'll get six of Kaliyana's most popular pieces, apt foundation for a new wardrobe for all four seasons. Simple complementary necklaces and comfy but übercool shoes are available, too. *4107 rue St-Denis.* ☎ 514/844-0633. *www.kaliyana.com. MC, V. Métro: Mont-Royal.*

★ **Kanuk** PLATEAU   One of the top Canadian manufacturers of high-end winter jackets makes its clothes right in Montréal. Like L.L. Bean in the U.S., Kanuk's first customers for the heavy parkas were outdoor enthusiasts. Today, its clientele includes the general public. The jackets aren't cheap—the heavy-duty ones cost upwards of C\$600—but they're extremely popular. The more modestly priced winter caps make nice (and cozy) souvenirs. *485 rue Rachel est.*

☎ 514/284-4494. www.kanuk.com. MC, V. Métro: Mont-Royal.

Mango DOWNTOWN An outlet of the ever-growing Spanish chain. Much of its merchandise consists of upmarket jeans and tees. The dressier separates intrigue with quiet tones and jazzy cuts—very Euro. *1000 rue Ste-Catherine ouest.* ☎ 514/397-2323. www.mango.com. AE, MC, V. Métro: Peel.

Moov Design PLATEAU Yoga enthusiasts seek out Moov's comfortable activewear. Even more intriguing is the option of having a bathing suit made-to-order within Montréal city limits. Customers choose the style and fabric that most complements their silhouette. *4148 bd. St-Laurent.* ☎ 514/658-9912. www.moovdesign.com. MC, V. Métro: Mont-Royal.

★ **Lola & Emily** PLATEAU One of the most popular boutiques for women's clothing in the Plateau. You'll find classic patterns with an alternative and feminine twist, in graceful and sleek dresses and asymmetrical

Roots is renowned for its stylish sportswear.

skirts. *3475 bd. St-Laurent.* ☎ 514/288-7598. www.lolaandemily.com. AE, MC, V. Métro: St-Laurent.

Roots DOWNTOWN This Canadian company has churned out stylish casual wear for the masses since 1973. Along with clothing, this three-floor store sells leather bags, briefcases, and home accessories. *1035 rue Ste-Catherine ouest.* ☎ 514/845-7995. www.roots.com. AE, MC, V. Métro: Peel.

Edibles

Frenco PLATEAU Your body will rejoice at this small health-food grocery. Whole grains, oats, wheat germ, and all sorts of fiber-rich foodstuffs are dispensed from plastic towers, and the organic and natural medicines behind the counter might ease the effects of a night of *poutine* or smoked meat. *3985 bd. St-Laurent.* ☎ 514/285-1319. MC, V. Métro: St-Laurent.

La Vieille Europe PLATEAU Create the mother of all picnic lunches with the wide selection of delectable cheeses and salty cold cuts found here. The gourmet fare is imported mostly from France, England, and Germany. *3855 bd. St-Laurent.* ☎ 514/842-5773. MC, V. Métro: St-Laurent.

kids Les Chocolats de Chloé PLATEAU If you approach chocolate the way certain aficionados approach wine or cheese—that is, on the lookout for the best of the best—then this tiny shop will bring great delight. Chocolates are made on-site, and tastes can be had for under C$2. *546 rue Duluth est.* ☎ 514/849-5550. www.leschocolatsdechloe.com. V. Métro: Mont-Royal.

★ **Marché Atwater** DOWNTOWN Atwater market, west of Old Montréal, is an indoor-outdoor farmer's market that's open daily. Very French in flavor, it features fresh fruits, vegetables and flowers, *boulangeries* and *fromageries*, plus shops with easy-to-travel-with food. *138 av. Atwater.* ☎ *514/937-7754. Most vendors don't take credit cards. Métro: Lionel-Groulx.*

SAQ DOWNTOWN Wine and spirits (although not beer) are heavily regulated by the provincial government and sold in SAQ outlets. The Express outlets offer the most popular libations and are open until 10pm, while the Signature outlets have the rarest and most expensive bottles. Consider Québec's unique ice cider *(cidre de glace)*, which is made from apples left on trees after the first frost. Domaine Pinnacle (www. icecider.com), based about an hour and a half from the city, is a regular gold medalist in international competitions. *SAQ Signature: 677 rue Ste-Catherine ouest.* ☎ *514/282-9445. www.saq.com. AE, MC, V. Métro: McGill.*

Suite 88 Chocolatier PLATEAU More fancy chocolates. These are displayed in cases like fine jewelry, with flavors that include jalapeño, chili cayenne, ouzo, and mojito. Small bars start at C$3.25. On cold days be sure to try the hot chocolate—it's made with cayenne. *3957 rue St-Denis.* ☎ *514/844-3488. www.suite88.com. AE, MC, V. Métro: Sherbrooke.*

Housewares
★ **Arthur Quentin** PLATEAU Doling out household products of quiet taste and discernment for more than 25 years, this St-Denis stalwart sells tableware, kitchen gadgets, and home decor, including Limoges china, tea towels, and copper pots.

Chocoholics have no shortage of options in Montréal.

3960 rue St-Denis. ☎ *514/843-7513. www.arthurquentin. com. AE, MC, V. Métro: Sherbrooke.*

★ **Bleu Nuit** PLATEAU A sister store to Arthur Quentin, above, Bleu Nuit is the place to go for natural fiber bedding, supersoft nightwear, and swank soaps. *3913 rue St-Denis (south of av. Duluth), Plateau Mont-Royal.* ☎ *514/843-5702. www.bleunuit.ca. AE, MC, V. Métro: Sherbrooke.*

kids Mortimer Snodgrass VIEUX-MONTREAL The unusual name should prepare shoppers for what's inside: loud vinyl handbags, quirky tools, children's clothing with humorous phrases emblazoned across the bum, and funky neon alarm clocks. You might not find a gift for that ultraconservative cousin of yours, but for everyone else Mortimer Snodgrass offers something

Mortimer Snodgrass is a prime spot for informal gifts.

A beautiful Inuit sculpture from Cape Dorset makes a wonderful memento.

that will make them smile. *209 rue St-Paul ouest.* ☎ *514/499-2851. www.mortimersnodgrass.com. MC, V. Métro: Place d'Armes.*

★ **kids Musée des Beaux-Arts Boutique** DOWNTOWN This unusually large and impressive shop sells everything from folk art to furniture. The expected art-related postcards and prints are on hand, along with ties, watches, scarves, address books, toys, jewelry, and Inuit crafts, with special focus on work by Québbec artisans. The boutique is also online in case you're looking for gifts after you've left the city. *1390 rue Sherbrooke ouest.* ☎ *514/285-1600. www.mbam.qc.ca. AE, MC, V. Métro: Peel.*

Music

Archambault Musique DOWN-TOWN There's a huge selection of English and French CDs on the ground floor, and a good variety of Québécois albums that you won't find outside of the province. *500 rue Ste-Catherine est.* ☎ *514/849-6201. www.archambault.ca. AE, MC, V. Métro: Berri-UQAM.*

Beatnick's PLATEAU The storefront at this everyman's record store hasn't changed much in the last decade, and its faithful customers return again and again. Selection is varied and you might be able to score that highly sought-after '60s release you've always wanted. *3770 rue St-Denis.* ☎ *514/842-0664. www. beatnickmusic.com. MC, V. Métro: Sherbrooke.*

Beatnick's is a prime spot for picking up old music releases.

Exploring the **Underground City**

If you'd like to visit Montréal's Underground City (a network of subterranean shops, cafes, and entrances to hotels and Métro stations), but you're intimidated about where to start, here's a minitour that hits five of the anchors. Keep in mind that no singular entity manages the network, which means that sections open and close according to hours set by the businesses, and maps, signage, and even the numbering of levels can differ from one section to the next. Persons using wheelchairs or strollers may face navigational challenges.

Place Ville-Marie. There is no prettier way to enter the underground than through one of I. M. Pei's glass pyramids in front of his famous crucifix-shaped office building, known locally as PVM. Built in 1962 to cover an unsightly railway trench north of Gare Central, the now-famous 41-story building became not just home to the city's first subterranean shopping mall but a cornerstone of the Underground City as well. Take the escalator down. You'll find a food court and shops, and several exits into the network. Look for the tunnel to Eaton Centre. *4 Place Ville-Marie.* ☎ *514/866-6666. www. placevillemarie.com.*

Le Centre Eaton. You'll know you're in Eaton Centre when you arrive at a courtyard and can look up at four floors of stores and restaurants and a scrape of sky through the glass-peaked roof. Eaton is the largest commercial space downtown and one of the most popular places in the pedestrian network. One local clothier described Eaton's ongoing appeal as "happy, happy, happy." Maybe it's that peep of sky? *705 rue Ste-Catherine ouest.*

Ticket counters at Gare Central.

☎ *514/288-3710. www.centreeaton demontreal.com.*

Les Cours Mont-Royal. From Eaton's courtyard, follow the signs to boulevard de Maisonneuve or to the Métro (you must go up from "level one tunnel" to "level two Métro"). You'll walk the equivalent of 3 short city blocks.

First Nations sculptures hang from the ceilings at Les Cours Mont-Royal, a fashionable mall.

Les Cours Mont-Royal has a distinct personality: A majority of its shops are independently owned, so cutting-edge fashion and trendy styles reign supreme. Some establishments cater to the young, moneyed, clubbing crowd while others to the chic, personal tailor crowd. There's a beautiful central chandelier (and some smaller ones in the food court) and six metal birdlike sculptures in permanent flight above the atrium made by First Nations artist David Piqtoukun. *1455 rue Peel.* ☎ *514/842-7777. www.lcmr.ca.*

Complex Les Ailes. Follow the signs from the Eaton Centre to the trilevel Complex Les Ailes, home to some of the city's most recognizable boutiques—Lacoste, Guess? and Swarovski, to name a few. The anchor store, Le Grand Magasin Ailes de la Mode, specializes in affordable family fashion. The landmark building in which the complex resides was built in 1927 for the now-departed Eaton's department store.

You can shop in the Underground City without having to worry about Montréal's fickle weather.

677 rue Ste-Catherine ouest. ☎ *514/ 288-3759. www.complexelesailes. com.*

Les Promenade de la Cathédrale. From Complex Les Aisles, follow the signs to Les Promenade de la Cathédrale to the site of one of Montréal's most unique architectural endeavors. The Cathédrale Christ Church (p 15), which sits above, was "floated" on supports as the arcades below were built. More than 8,200 tons (18 million lbs.) had to be stabilized for the duration of construction, and architects, historians, and artisans dismantled the cathedral's presbytery stone by stone then reconstructed it exactly as before. Look for photographs depicting the process in the halls of this mall. *625 rue Ste-Catherine.* ☎ *514/849-9925. www.promenades cathedrale.com.* ●

The Place Montréal Trust mall is one of the many retail developments that make up Montréal's famous Underground City.

Dining Best Bets

Chez l'Epicier is one of the best places in the city for innovative comfort food.

Best **New Restaurant**
★★ DNA $$$$ 355 rue Marguerite D'Youville (p 96)

Best **Place to Drop C$100**
★★★ Europea $$$$$ 1227 rue de la Montagne (p 96)

Best **Paris-Style Bistro**
★ L'Express $$ 3927 rue St-Denis (p 95)

Best **Outdoor Patio**
★ Boris Bistro $$ 465 rue McGill (p 96)

Best **Québécois**
★★ Aix Cuisine du Terroir $$$$ 711 Côte de la Place d'Armes (p 96)

Best **Seafood**
★★★ Ferreira Café $$$$ 1446 rue Peel (p 96)

Best **Slabs of Pork**
★★ Au Pied de Cochon $$$ 536 rue Duluth (p 95)

Best **Vegan**
★ Aux Vivres $ 4631 bd. St-Laurent (p 95)

Best **Dependable Breakfast**
Eggspectation $ 201 rue St-Jacques ouest (p 96)

Best **Indian**
★ Gandhi $$ 230 rue St-Paul ouest (p 96)

Best **Polish**
Stash Café $$ 200 rue St-Paul ouest (p 96)

Best **24-Hour Poutine**
★ La Banquise $ 994 rue Rachel est (p 95)

Best **Sandwich**
★ Olive et Gourmando $ 351 rue St-Paul est (p 96)

Best **Bakery**
★ Premiere Moisson $ 1490 rue Sherbrooke ouest (p 96)

Best **Creative Cuisine**
★★★ Toque! $$$$$ 900 Place Jean-Paul-Riopelle (p 96)

Best **Fast Food on Rue Crescent**
Boustan $ 2020A rue Crescent (p 96)

Best **Raw Industrial Setting**
Cluny ArtBar $ 257 rue Prince (p 96)

Best **Bring-Your-Own-Wine Resto**
★ L'Academie $$ 4051 rue St-Denis (p 95)

Best **Vegetarian Buffet**
Le Commensal $ 1204 av. McGill College (p 96)

Best **Oysters**
★ Maestro S.V.P. $$$ 3615 bd. St-Laurent (p 95)

Best **Bagels**
★★★ St-Viateur Bagels $ 1127 av. Mont-Royal (p 95); and Fairmont Bagel $ 74 av. Fairmont ouest (p 95)

Best **Smoked Meat**
★ Schwartz's $ 3895 bd. St-Laurent (p 95)

Previous page: A gourmet dish from the kitchen at the Fairmont The Queen Elizabeth hotel.

Dining in the Plateau

Au Pied de Cochon 10
Aux Vivres 5
Globe 1
L'Academie 9
L'Express 11
La Banquise 8
Maestro S.V.P. 2
Patati Patata 4
Schwartz's 3
St-Viateur Bagels 7
Fairmont Bagel 6

Metro Station

Dining in Centre-Ville & Vieux-Montréal

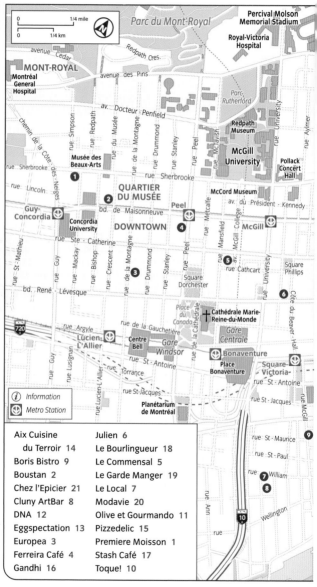

Aix Cuisine du Terroir 14
Boris Bistro 9
Boustan 2
Chez l'Epicier 21
Cluny ArtBar 8
DNA 12
Eggspectation 13
Europea 3
Ferreira Café 4
Gandhi 16
Julien 6
Le Bourlingueur 18
Le Commensal 5
Le Garde Manger 19
Le Local 7
Modavie 20
Olive et Gourmando 11
Pizzedelic 15
Premiere Moisson 1
Stash Café 17
Toque! 10

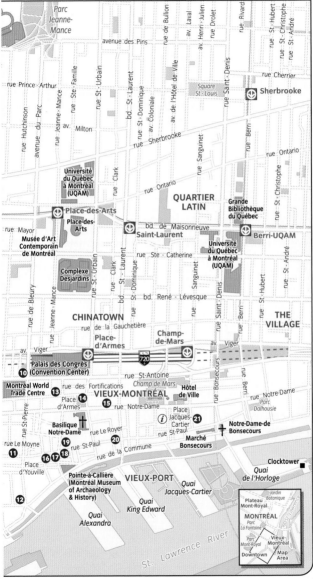

Restaurants **A to Z**

★★ Aix Cuisine du Terroir

VIEUX-MONTREAL *CONTEMPORARY QUEBECOIS* The sophisticated flavors found in this restaurant's excellent regional preparations of fish, boar, and duck have justifiably garnered critical praise. Add in the upscale decor and an intelligent waitstaff, and you have the ingredients for an exquisite dining experience. *711 Côte de la Place d'Armes (in the Hotel Place d'Armes).* ☎ *514/904-1201. www.aixcuisine.com. Entrees C$26–C$45. AE, DC, DISC, MC, V. Lunch & dinner daily. Métro: Place d'Armes. Map p 97.*

★★ Au Pied de Cochon PLA-

TEAU *QUEBECOIS* Some of the best meals at "the Pig's Foot" unsurprisingly feature cuts of pork, though massive amounts of beef, chicken, lamb, duck, and venison are also used to create artery-clogging dishes that are sinfully delectable. This legendary place fills up quickly during normal dining hours. *536 rue Duluth.* ☎ *514/281-1116. www.restaurantaupieddecochon.ca. Reservations recommended. Entrees C$19–C$45. AE, MC, V. Dinner Tues–Sun. Métro: Sherbrooke. Map p 95.*

★ Aux Vivres PLATEAU *VEGAN*

Carnivores won't notice that the fresh and tasty dishes here are all missing meat (and all other animal products). A large menu includes bowls of chili with guacamole, bok choi with grilled tofu and peanut sauce, and yummy desserts. *4631 bd. St-Laurent.* ☎ *514/842-3479. Most items under C$12. No credit cards. Lunch & dinner Tues–Sun. Map p 95.*

★ Boris Bistro VIEUX-MONTREAL

BISTRO The outdoor patio here stands out as especially pretty, with leafy trees, large umbrellas, and, at night, subtle lighting and candles. French fries cooked in duck fat are a signature dish, and there's a choice of about a half-dozen *fromages du terroir,* local cheeses, to close a meal. *465 rue McGill.* ☎ *514/848-9575. www.borisbistro.com. Entrees C$14–C$20. AE, MC, V. Lunch & dinner daily in summer, limited hrs. in winter. Métro: Peel. Map p 96.*

Boustan DOWNTOWN *LEBANESE*

In the middle of the hubbub among the bars and clubs on rue Crescent, this Lebanese eatery, completely nondescript and consistently popular, has a line out the door at 2pm (office workers) and again at 2am (late-night partiers), all jonesing for its famed falafel, *shish taouk,* and

For exceptional dining in Vieux-Montréal, head to Aix Cuisine du Terroir.

shawarma sandwiches. *2020A rue Crescent.* ☎ *514/843-3576. Most items under C$10. MC, V. Lunch & dinner until 4am Mon–Sat, dinner until 4am Sun. Métro: Peel. Map p 96.*

★ **Chez l'Epicier** VIEUX-MONTREAL *FUSION*   For an interesting combination of innovation and comfort food, head to this atmospheric haunt, one of Montréal's most inventive and original restaurants. It's frequented by diners looking for international twists on familiar French dishes, such as *rösti* made of sweet potato and Asian spices. Don't leave without sampling the decadent dessert menu. *331 rue St-Paul est.* ☎ *514/878-2232. Entrees C$27–C$40. AE, MC, V. Lunch & dinner Mon–Fri, dinner Sat–Sun. Métro: Champ-de-Mars. Map p 96.*

Cluny ArtBar VIEUX-MONTREAL *LIGHT FARE*   Though it's called a bar, Cluny's main hours are during the daylight, when the sun streams in through mammoth industrial windows. This appealing cafe is inside the Darling Foundry, an avant-garde exhibition space in a vast, raw, former foundry, located in the loft-and-factory district west of avenue McGill. Cluny serves up coffee, croissants, and lunch, with fare such as vegetarian antipasto, cream of parsnip soup, and smoked salmon panini. *257 rue Prince.* ☎ *514/866-1213. www.fonderiedarling.org/louer_e/cluny.html. Entrees C$4–C$19. MC, V. Breakfast & lunch Mon–Fri, dinner Thurs. Métro: Square Victoria. Map p 96.*

★★ **DNA** VIEUX-MONTREAL *CONTEMPORARY QUEBECOIS*   Blazing onto the Montréal restaurant scene in 2008, DNA suffuses concept dining with affable, expert service. Wondering about the origin of the fiddleheads or nettles? Servers will carry a basket of fresh and locally-grown ingredients to your table for

Meals at Aux Vivres are both nutritious and delicious.

a gastronomic dialogue. Glass slabs divide the restaurant into nooks that allow the excitement of a packed house to bubble over without sacrificing intimacy. *355 rue Marguerite D'Youville.* ☎ *514/287-3362. www.dnarestaurant.com. Entrees C$24–C$36, 5-course tasting menu C$85. AE, MC, V. Lunch & dinner Tues–Fri, dinner Sat–Sun. Métro: Square Victoria. Map p 96.*

Eggspectation VIEUX-MONTREAL *BREAKFAST/LIGHT FARE*   The atmosphere and food here are funky and creative, and prices are fair for the large portions. What's more, the kitchen knows how to deal with volume and turns out good meals in nearly lightning speed, even on packed weekend mornings. There are eight variations of eggs Benedict alone. This is a chain ("constantly eggspanding," as they put it), with eight Montréal locations in addition to this one. *201 rue St-Jacques ouest.* ☎ *514/282-0119. www.eggspectation.ca. Most items under C$12. AE, MC, V. Breakfast & lunch daily. Métro: Place d'Armes. Map p 96.*

★★★ **Europea** DOWNTOWN *CONTEMPORARY FRENCH*   Chef Jérôme Ferrer is one of the biggest stars in the city, and Europea consistently wins accolades from the local media

Cluny ArtBar serves up tasty cafe fare in a funky industrial setting.

for his concoctions. Even the "teasers" are fun, such as a demitasse of lobster cream cappuccino with truffle shavings. For the full treatment, order the 10-course menu degustation for C$87. For a bargain, come at lunch, when the *table d'hôte* starts at C$21. *1227 rue de la Montagne.* 📞 *514/398-9229. Reservations recommended. Entrees C$30–C$44. AE, DC, MC, V. Lunch & dinner Tues–Fri, dinner Sat–Sun. Métro: Peel. Map p 96.*

★★★ **Ferreira Café** DOWNTOWN *SEAFOOD/PORTUGUESE* To quote *Montréal Gazette* food critic Lesley Chesterman, "Downtown Montréal may not be the coolest dining destination anymore, but at Ferreira on a sunny Friday night, I can think of few restaurants more impressive." Indeed, the food is excellent—the cataplana stew is a highlight—and the Portuguese decor is both festive and sexy. *1446 rue Peel.* 📞 *514/848-0988. www.ferreiracafe.com. Reservations recommended. Entrees C$26–C$40. AE, MC, V. Lunch & dinner Mon–Fri, dinner Sat. Métro: Peel. Map p 96.*

★ **Gandhi** VIEUX-MONTREAL *INDIAN* The always busy but wonderfully cozy Gandhi won't disappoint with its usual Indian fare (chicken tandoori, *tikka,* and so on). Little twists on their interesting curries will leave your taste buds tingling. *230 rue St-Paul ouest.* 📞 *514/845-5866. www.restaurantgandhi.com. Entrees*

C$10–C$20. Lunch & dinner Mon–Fri, dinner Sat–Sun. Métro: Place d'Armes. Map p 96.

★ **Globe** PLATEAU *ITALIAN* The waitstaff and clientele, in true St-Laurent style, are eye candy for the executives who frequent this pricey but trendy spot. The food on the ever-changing menu is solid enough to justify the hefty price tags. *3455 bd. St-Laurent.* 📞 *514/284-3823. www.restaurantglobe.com. Reservations recommended. Entrees C$24–C$49. AE, DC, MC, V. Dinner daily. Métro: St-Laurent. Map p 95.*

Julien DOWNTOWN *TRADITIONAL FRENCH* This relaxed Parisian-style bistro hosts businesspeople at lunch and for after-work cocktails and mostly tourists from nearby hotels in the evening. The menu offers generous-size portions of classics such as mussels with fries, and there's always a vegetarian pasta option, too. Much of the year, diners have the option of sitting at tables on the heated terrace. *1191 av. Union.* 📞 *514/871-1581. www.restaurantjulien.com. Entrees C$17–C$31. AE, MC, V. Lunch & dinner Mon–Fri, dinner Sat. Métro: Square Victoria. Map p 96.*

★ **La Banquise** PLATEAU *LIGHT FARE* Open 24 hours a day on Parc La Fontaine's north end, this friendly, hippy-meets-hipster diner is a city landmark for its *poutine,* with some two dozen variations on the standard french fries with gravy and cheese curds. Add-ons range from smoked sausage to hot peppers to smoked meat to bacon. The chefs use real cheese curds instead of regular cheese, and the gravy is among the tastiest in town. *994 rue Rachel est.* 📞 *514/525-2415. www.restolabanquise.com. Poutine plates C$6–C$10, most other items under C$11. No credit cards. Open 24 hr. daily. Map p 95.*

★ **L'Academie** PLATEAU *MEDITER-RANEAN* The top "Bring Your Own Wine" destination on rue St-Denis has a modern, upscale decor, but those in casual wear won't feel out of place. Grab a bottle from the SAQ next door and order one of the excellent pasta dishes or a plate of *moule et frites* (mussels and fries). There's also an outpost downtown at 2100 rue Crescent. *4051 rue St-Denis. ☎ 514/849-2249. www.lacademie.ca. Entrees C$14–C$28. AE, MC, V. Lunch & dinner daily. Métro: Sherbrooke. Map p 95.*

Le Bourlingueur VIEUX-MON-TREAL *TRADITIONAL FRENCH* The advantage here is price: The restaurant charges unbelievably low prices for several four-course meals daily. The blackboard menu changes depending on what's available at the market that day. Roast pork with applesauce, glazed duck leg, and *choucroute garnie* (sauerkraut with meat) are likely to show up, but the house specialty is seafood—look for the shrimp in Pernod sauce. *363 rue St-Francois-Xavier. ☎ 514/845-3646. www.lebourlingueur.ca. Reservations recommended Sat–Sun. Entrees and table d'hôte lunch & dinner C$12–C$22. MC, V. Lunch & dinner daily. Métro: Place d'Armes. Map p 96.*

Le Commensal DOWNTOWN *VEGETARIAN* Choose from a huge selection of hot and cold dishes at this buffet-style vegetarian restaurant and pay by the weight. Even with the cafeteria feel, both presentation and flavor make this an appealing option. *1204 av. McGill College. ☎ 514/871-1480. www. commensal.com. Most meals under C$10. AE, MC, V. Lunch & dinner daily. Métro: McGill. Map p 96.*

Le Garde Manger VIEUX-MON-TREAL *SEAFOOD* From the dark roadhouse decor to the rowdy slip of a bar, this giddy resto is a smack down to its gentrified Vieux-Mon-tréal neighbors. On the plus side, food like spicy jerk snow crab or lobster *poutine* is pretty good and generously portioned. You'll need a lead stomach to survive a whole portion of the signature dessert, a fried Mars bar, unless deafening rock music helps you digest. *408 rue St-François-Xavier. ☎ 514/678-5044. Reservations recommended. Entrees C$25–C$35. AE, MC, V. Dinner Tues–Sat. Métro: Place d'Armes. Map p 96.*

★★ **Le Local** VIEUX-MONTREAL *CONTEMPORARY FRENCH* Chef Charles-Emmanuel Pariseau trained locally before opening these doors in 2008, and his kitchen breathes new life into standards like surf and turf (theirs has barbecue ribs). Sample menu item: puff pastry tart with

The popular L'Academie is the city's top BYOB restaurant.

Bargain Hunters: Look for the *Table d'Hôte*

Always consider the *table d'hôte* meals at restaurants. Ubiquitous in Montréal, they are fixed-price menus with three or four courses, and they usually cost just a little more than the price of a single a la carte main course. Restaurants at all price ranges offer them, and they represent the best value around. *Table d'hôte* meals are often offered not just at dinner but at lunch, too, when they are even less expensive. Having your main meal midday instead of in the evening is the most economical way to sample many of the top establishments.

Prices listed in this chapter do not include the *table d'hôte* options, so you may be able to dine for significantly less than these prices indicate.

roasted scallops, chorizo, and blood pudding. *740 rue William.* ☎ *514/397-7737. www.resto-lelocal.com. Reservations recommended. Entrees C$19–C$31. MC, V. Lunch & dinner Mon–Fri, dinner Sat–Sun. Métro: Square Victoria. Map p 96.*

★ **L'Express** PLATEAU *BISTRO* No obvious sign announces L'Express, perhaps because tout Montréal knows exactly where this most classic of Parisian-style bistros is. Eternally busy and open until 3am, the bistro's atmosphere hits all the right notes: checkered floor, high ceiling,

Pizzadelic is noted for its quirky toppings and delicious pizzas.

mirrored walls, *soupe de poisson,* and croque-monsieur. Single diners and walk-ins can often find a seat at the zinc-topped bar. *3927 rue St-Denis.* ☎ *514/845-5333. Reservations recommended. Entrees C$10–C$23. AE, DC, MC, V. Breakfast, lunch & dinner daily. Métro: Sherbrooke. Map p 95.*

Maestro S.V.P. PLATEAU *SEAFOOD* Smaller and more relaxed than other restaurants in the 2 blocks of St-Laurent north of Sherbrooke, the highlight of this bistro is its oysters, which staff are happy to walk you through. A 40-item tapas menu tantalizes Tuesday through Friday from 11am until 5pm, as well as all night on Tuesday and Wednesday, with most plates under C$10. An all-you-can-eat mussel special is available on Sunday and Monday nights for C$13. *3615 bd. St-Laurent.* ☎ *514/842-6447. www.maestrosvp. com. Reservations recommended. Entrees C$16–C$75, most under C$35. AE, DC, MC, V. Lunch & dinner Tues–Fri, dinner Sat–Mon. Métro: Sherbrooke. Map p 95.*

★ **Modavie** VIEUX-MONTREAL *MEDITERRANEAN* The real treat

here is the lamb options (there are six), but other great choices include tiger shrimp in grand marnier sauce and ravioli stuffed with goat cheese. Live jazz is presented nightly from 7 until about 10pm. *1 rue St-Paul ouest.* ☎ *514/287-9582. www.modavie.com. Reservations recommended. Entrees C$17–C$49. AE, MC, V. Lunch & dinner daily. Métro: Place d'Armes. Map p 96.*

★ **Olive et Gourmando** VIEUX-MONTRÉAL *SANDWICHES/LIGHT FARE* A local favorite. It started out as an earthy bakery, added table service, and transformed into a full-fledged cafe. Croissants, scones, biscuits, and creative sandwiches are all good—maybe smoked trout with capers, sun-dried tomatoes, spinach, and herbed cream cheese on grilled bread? *351 rue St-Paul ouest.* ☎ *514/350-1083. www.oliveetgourmando.com. Most itemsunder C$10. No credit cards. Breakfast & lunch until 6pm Tues–Sat. Métro: Square-Victoria. Map p 96.*

★ **Patati Patata** PLATEAU *LIGHT FARE* Tiny burgers, tiny prices, tiny space. This friendly nook seats no more than a dozen patrons at a time, but lining up to take a spot pays off with top-notch breakfasts, burgers, and *poutine. 4177 bd. St-Laurent.* ☎ *514/844-0216. Most items under C$7. No credit cards. Breakfast, lunch & dinner daily. Map p 95.*

kids Pizzedelic VIEUX-MONTRÉAL *PIZZA* Thanks to ingredients such as pickled ginger and mandarin orange, this is not your typical pizza. The quirky combinations are both interesting and delectable. There's also a location at 3467 bd.

Premiere Moisson sells more than 40 varieties of bread and is one of the best spots in town for picnic supplies.

St-Laurent about a block north of rue Sherbrooke. *39 rue Notre-Dame ouest.* ☎ *514/286-1200. www.pizzedelic-montreal.com. Pizzas and pastas C$8.50–C$17. MC, V. Lunch & dinner daily. Métro: Place d'Armes. Map p 96.*

★ **Premiere Moisson** DOWNTOWN *BAKERY* Montréal's best bakery (there are multiple branches scattered throughout the city) got its reputation by crafting over 40 varieties of breads and baguettes. It also serves up sandwiches and mind-boggling pastries. *1490 rue Sherbrooke ouest.* ☎ *514/931-6540. www.premieremoisson.com. Most items under C$12. MC, V. Breakfast, lunch & dinner daily. Métro: Guy-Concordia. Map p 96.*

★★★ **St-Viateur Bagels** PLATEAU *BAKERY/LIGHT FARE* Famous around the world for their dense, sweet dough, Montréal's oven-fired bagels have gained much of their renown thanks to St-Viateur's. This small shop in the Plateau has been boiling bagels in honeyed water and baking them since 1957. Don't leave the city without sampling a few straight from the oven. Competitor Fairmont Bagel is located at 74 av. Fairmont ouest and is open 24 hours a day, 365 days a year. *1127 av. Mont-Royal.* ☎ *514/528-6361. www.stviateurbagel.com. Most items under C$12, individual bagels C$.60 each. No credit cards. Breakfast, lunch & dinner daily. Métro: Mont-Royal. Map p 95.*

★ **Schwartz's** PLATEAU *DELI* This legendary Montréal eatery is

Say Cheese, Please

The cheeses of Québec are renowned for their rich flavors and textures, and many can only be sampled in Canada because they are often unpasteurized—made of *lait cru* (raw milk)—and therefore subject to strict export law. When dining in Montréal, do yourself a favor and order some as a final course. Choices include the buttery St-Basil de Port Neuf; Le Chèvre Noire, a sharp goats-milk variety that's covered in black wax; and the creamy Blue Ermite, made by monks at an Abbaye 2 hours west of the city (p 152).

Cheeses with the *fromages de pays* label are made in Québec with no modified milk ingredients. The label represents solidarity among artisanal producers and is supported by Solidarité Rurale du Québec, a group devoted to revitalizing rural communities. It's also supported by Slow Food Québec, which promotes sustainable agriculture and local production. Information is available at www.fromage duquebec.qc.ca.

Montréal's restaurants are notable for their vast array of cheese selections; be sure to sample a few when dining out.

crowded, waiters are brusque, the counter is a mess, and the line can reach the end of the block. Still, many are convinced it's the only place to indulge in the guilty treat of *viande fumée*—a kind of brisket that's called, simply, smoked meat. Most people also order sides of fries and mammoth garlicky pickles. *3895 bd. St-Laurent.* ☎ *514/842-4813. www.schwartzsdeli.com. Sandwiches and meat plates C$5–C$17. No credit cards. Breakfast, lunch & dinner daily. Métro: Sherbrooke. Map p 95.*

Stash Café VIEUX-MONTREAL *POLISH* At this site for almost 30 years, this *restauracja polska* draws throngs of enthusiastic returnees for its abundant offerings and low prices. Roast wild boar has long been featured, along with *bigos* (a cabbage-and-meat stew), pirogi (dumplings stuffed with meat,

cheese, or cabbage), and potato pancakes. A jolly tone prevails, with such menu admonitions as "anything tastes better with wodka, even wodka." *200 rue St-Paul ouest.* ☎ *514/845-6611. www.stashcafe. com. Entrees C$11–C$17. AE, DC, MC, V. Lunch & dinner daily. Métro: Place d'Armes. Map p 96.*

★★★ Toque! DOWNTOWN *CONTEMPORARY FRENCH* The celebrated Toque! overwhelms with unparalleled service and dazzling cuisine. Opt for one of the tasting menus to ease the decision-making process and to better sample the famed kitchen's amazing creations. *900 Place Jean-Paul-Riopelle.* ☎ *514/499-2084. www.restaurant-toque.com. Reservations required. Entrees C$41–C$47, tasting menus C$92 or C$104. AE, DC, MC, V. Dinner Tues–Sat. Métro: Sherbrooke. Map p 96.* ●

The Best Nightlife

Nightlife Best Bets

La Cage Aux Sports, the best bar in town for watching a Canadiens game.

Best **Local Beer Selection**
★ Brutopia, *1219 rue Crescent* (p 110)

Best **People-Watching**
★ Le St-Sulpice, *1680 rue St-Denis* (p 111)

Best **Hipster Bar**
★★ Bílý Kůň, *354 av. Mont-Royal est* (p 110)

Best **Chic New Wine Bar**
★ Chesterfield Bar à Vin, *451 rue Rachel est* (p 111)

Best **Downtown Wine Bar**
★ Pullman, *3424 av. du Parc* (p 112)

Best **Bar for a Huge Group**
★ Sir Winston Churchill Pub, *1459 rue Crescent* (p 112)

Best **Irish Pub**
Hurley's Irish Pub, *1225 rue Crescent* (p 113)

Best **Bar to Watch the Habs Play**
La Cage Aux Sports, *1437 bd. René Lévesque ouest* (p 111)

Best **Sports Bar Overall**
Champs, *3956 bd. St-Laurent* (p 110)

Best **Hidden Corner for Romance**
★ Le Sainte Élisabeth Pub Européan, *1412 rue St-Elisabeth* (p 111)

Best **Bar for 20-Somethings**
Le Pistol, *3723 bd. St-Laurent* (p 111)

Best **Gay Bar**
Sky Club & Pub, *1474 rue Ste-Catherine est* (p 112)

Best **Dance Club**
★★ Tokyo Bar, *3709 bd. St-Laurent* (p 112)

Best **Drag Club**
Cabaret Mado, *1115 rue Ste-Catherine est* (p 113)

Best **Bar to See Indie Rock**
★ La Sala Rosa, *4848 bd. St-Laurent* (p 114)

Best **Old-School Jazz Club**
★ Maison du Jazz, *2060 rue Aylmer* (p 114)

Best **Low-Key Jazz Venue**
★ Upstairs Jazz Bar & Grill, *1254 rue Mackay* (p 114)

Best **Celebrity Spotting**
★ Buonanotte, *3518 bd. St-Laurent* (p 110)

Best **Cocktail Bar**
Koko, *8 rue Sherbrooke ouest* (p 111)

Best **Dive Bar**
Biftek, *3702 bd. St-Laurent* (p 110)

Best **Late-Night Menu in Sexy Setting**
★★★ Ferreira Café, *1446 rue Peel* (p 100)

Best **Paris-Style Bistro Open Until 3am**
★ L'Express, *3927 rue St-Denis* (p 102)

Previous page: Musicians play at Montréal's famed International Festival of Jazz.

Nightlife in Plateau Mont-Royal & the Village

Biftek **7**
Bilý Kůň **2**
Buonanotte **9**
Cabaret Mado **15**
Casa del Popolo **1**
Champs **4**
Chesterfield Bar
  à Vin **3**
Club Balattou **1**
Club Opera **11**
Club Soda **12**
Koko **10**
La Sala Rosa **1**
Le Divan Orange **1**
Le Pistol **5**
Le St-Sulpice **14**
Le Sainte Élisabeth
  Pub Européan **13**
Orchid **8**
Sky Club & Pub **16**
Tokyo Bar **6**

Nightlife in Downtown Montréal

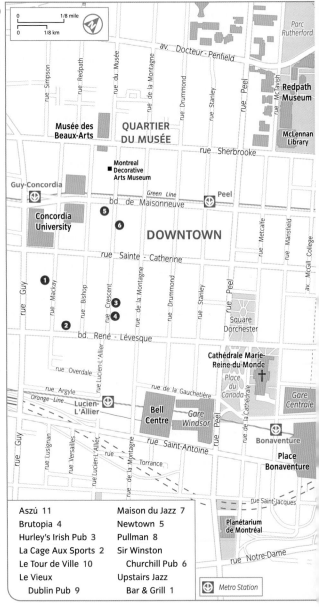

Aszú 11	Maison du Jazz 7
Brutopia 4	Newtown 5
Hurley's Irish Pub 3	Pullman 8
La Cage Aux Sports 2	Sir Winston
Le Tour de Ville 10	Churchill Pub 6
Le Vieux	Upstairs Jazz
Dublin Pub 9	Bar & Grill 1

◉ Metro Station

Montréal **Nightlife A to Z**

Bars

Aszú VIEUX-MONTREAL This classy wine bar features hundreds of labels, with some 50 of them available by the glass each evening. A menu of tuna tartar, Québécois guinea fowl, wild boar chop, and the like provides accompaniment. *212 rue Notre-Dame ouest. 514/ 845-5436. www.aszu.ca. Métro: Place d'Armes. Map p 108.*

Biftek PLATEAU A grungy crowd aging from barely legal to early 30s holds court at this perennially popular bar. Play a game of pool or just kick back listening to the city's best rotation of indie and classic rock. *3702 bd. St-Laurent. 514/844-6211. Métro: Sherbrooke. Map p 107.*

★★ Bilý Kůň PLATEAU Pronounced "Billy Coon," this is a bit of Prague right in Montréal. Decor is avant-garde and drink options include Czech beers and martini specials such as Absinthe Aux Pommes. Students and professionals jam in for the relaxed candlelit atmosphere. There's live jazz from 6 to 8pm nightly and DJs spinning upbeat pop most evenings from 8pm to 3am. *354 av. Mont-Royal est (near rue St-Denis). 514/ 845-5392. www.bilykun.com. Métro: Mont-Royal. Map p 107.*

★ Brutopia DOWNTOWN Beer aficionados will love Brutopia's own homebrewed beer and its collection of other Québec microbrews. Unlike other spots on rue Crescent, where the sound levels can be deafening, here you can actually have a conversation. *1219 rue Crescent. 514/ 393-9277. www.brutopia.net. Métro: Lucien-L'Allier. Map p 108.*

★ Buonanotte PLATEAU This is a super high-end, expensive Italian restaurant, and as night rolls on and the music gets louder, the impossibly attractive clientele shifts closer to both the bar and each other. If you're not a regular, you might get shut out if you show up after 11pm. *3518 bd. St-Laurent. 514/848-0644. www.buonanotte.com. Métro: St-Laurent. Map p 107.*

Champs PLATEAU The best place to catch a major sporting event, and often packed. Flatscreen TVs are posted everywhere so you don't miss any action. Settle into a booth for sports-friendly (if somewhat pricey) munchies and pints of Molson. *3956 bd. St-Laurent. 514/987-6444. www.champssportsbar.ca. Métro: Sherbrooke. Map p 107.*

Enjoy live music by candlelight at Bily Kůň.

★ **Chesterfield Bar à Vin** PLA-TEAU   Stop in for a glass of wine and you could find yourself veering off the nibbles menu and dining instead on lobsters and a crisp whole bottle of vino. In warmer months the windows open to rue Rachel and the bar heats up with DJs. *451 rue Rachel est.* 📞 *514/544-5316. www.chesterfieldmtl.com. Métro: Mont-Royal. Map p 107.*

Koko PLATEAU   One of the chic bars of the city. There's a spectacular terrace and an Asian-influenced menu, and it's open until 3am Thursday through Saturday (until 1am Sun–Wed). As befits its positioning as a premier venue for urban glamour, a bouncer often stands watch at the door. Try the C$12 Wilde Child cocktail, with prosecco and candied wild hibiscus flower. *8 rue Sherbrooke ouest.* 📞 *514/657-5656. www.kokomontreal.com. Métro: St-Laurent. Map p 107.*

La Cage Aux Sports DOWN-TOWN   The city's other big sports bar option. Part of a national chain, this outpost is home to some of the rowdiest Canadiens fans around. During the hockey season, you'll find yourself surrounded by a sea of red, white, and blue jerseys. *1437 bd. René Lévesque ouest.* 📞 *514/878-2243. www.cage.ca. Métro: Lucien-L'Allier. Map p 108.*

Le Pistol PLATEAU   Get here early, because this spot on the Main gets packed. Catering to the postcollegiate, T-shirt-and-jeans crowd, Pistol offers ample attractions, including high-definition plasma TVs showing hockey, tasty food, and music that moves from jazz to house to rock. *3723 bd. St-Laurent.* 📞 *514/847-2222. Métro: Sherbrooke. Map p 107.*

★ **Le St-Sulpice** QUARTIER LATIN   A four-story, immensely popular bar. It's Montréal's version of a Munich beer garden, set in a converted mansion that has a bookshelf-laden alcove, a street-side terrace, a pool-table area, and dance floors on the top floor and in the basement. In summer and on warm spring nights, the gigantic outdoor terrace in the back is one of the busiest and noisiest places on St-Denis. *1680 rue St-Denis.* 📞 *514/844-9458. www.lesaintsulpice.ca. Métro: Berri-UQAM. Map p 107.*

★ **Le Sainte Elisabeth Pub Européan** QUARTIER LATIN   This small and popular publike bar has one of the best outdoor terraces in town—three surrounding walls, covered in ivy, stretch high into the Montréal sky as strategically placed lights make you forget you're anywhere close to an unsavory part of rue Ste-Catherine. It's open even in the winter, when scattered heat lamps keep patrons warm. *1412 rue Ste-Elisabeth.* 📞 *514/286-4302. www.ste-elisabeth.com. Métro: Berri-UQAM. Map p 107.*

Le Tour de Ville DOWNTOWN   Montréal's only revolving restaurant and bar (the bar part doesn't revolve, but you still get a great view) . Go when the sun is setting and the city lights are beginning to blink on. *In the Delta Centre-Ville hotel, 777 rue University.* 📞 *514/879-4777. Métro: Square Victoria. Map p 108.*

★ **Le Vieux Dublin Pub** DOWN-TOWN   This cheerful old Irish pub is cozy and rarely gets crowded. There's occasional live music and a U.K.-influenced playlist featuring bands such as Belle & Sebastian, plus—naturally—pints of Harp Lager and excellent single-malt scotch. *1219A rue University.* 📞 *514/861-4448. Métro: McGill. Map p 108.*

Newtown DOWNTOWN   A trendy multilevel nightspot that's an oasis for the young, flirty, and sharply dressed. There's a disco in the basement, a restaurant one floor up, and, most prominently, a rooftop terrace in summer. *1476 rue Crescent.* ☎ *514/284-6555. www.lenewtown. com. Métro: Peel. Map p 108.*

★ **Pullman** DOWNTOWN This sleek wine bar offers either 2- or 4-ounce pours, so there is room for adventure. A competent tapas menu with standards like grilled cheese bedazzled with port and charcuterie are prepared with the precision of a sushi chef. The multilevel space creates pockets of ambience, from cozy corners to tables drenched in natural light. *3424 av. du Parc.* ☎ *514/288-7779. www. pullman-mtl.com. Métro: Place des Arts. Map p 108.*

★ **Sir Winston Churchill Pub** DOWNTOWN One of rue Crescent's prime mingling spots, this gigantic landmark is where singles come to sip martinis or beer after a rough day at work. *1459 rue Crescent.* ☎ *514/ 288-3814. www.swcpc.com. Métro: Guy-Concordia. Map p 108.*

Dance Clubs

★ **Club Opera** QUARTIER LATIN One of the hottest dance clubs in the city, attracting the thin, the tanned, and the well turned out. The club has an elegant ambience and international DJs spinning nearly every evening. *32 rue Ste-Catherine.* ☎ *514/842-2836. www.operamtl. com. Cover from C$15. Métro: St-Laurent. Map p 107.*

Orchid PLATEAU Wonder where Montréal's fine black professionals hang out? Their choice is the Orchid nightclub, and the lines here are as long as any on the Main. Dress to impress if you want to get in. *3556 bd. St-Laurent.* ☎ *514/848-6398. www. orchidnightclub.com. Cover up to C$15. Métro: Sherbrooke. Map p 107.*

The Village is a fun, fabulous nightlife destination.

★ **Sky Club & Pub** THE VILLAGE This is a complex that includes drag performances in the cabaret room, a pub serving dinner daily from 4 to 9pm, a hip-hop room, a spacious dance floor that's often set to house music, and a popular roof terrace. Sky is thought by many to be the city's top spot for the gay, young, and fabulous. *1474 rue Ste-Catherine est.* ☎ *514/529-6969. www.complexe sky.com. Métro: Beaudry. Map p 107.*

★★ **Tokyo Bar** PLATEAU This classy dance club—one of the best in Montréal—plays everything from hip-hop to disco for a mix of well-dressed regulars and tourists in their 20s and 30s. There's a rooftop terrace, a friendly and good-looking staff, a separate chill-out lounge, a dance floor, and a room that sometimes features live music or a DJ. *3709 bd. St-Laurent.* ☎ *514/842-6838. www.tokyobar. com. Cover C$7–C$10. Métro: Sherbrooke. Map p 107.*

Music Venues

The Festival International de Jazz de Montréal is one of the monster events on the city's calendar. The 2009 edition featured performances by Tony

Bennett, Ben Harper, and Dave Brubeck. It costs serious money to hear stars of such magnitude, and tickets sell out months in advance. Fortunately, 450 free outdoor performances also take place during the 11-day July party, many right on downtown's streets and plazas. Visit www.montrealjazzfest.com or call ☎ 888/515-0515 or 514/871-1881 for information. Another big festival is Bal en Blanc Party Week, a 5-day rave/dance party over Easter weekend in April that's one of the biggest such events in the world. In 2009, an estimated 15,000 people came out for the house and trace DJ events at Palais des Congrès and smaller clubs. Visit www.balenblanc.com for more information. Also see "Sports and Rock Venues," in chapter 7, p 121.

Cabaret Mado THE VILLAGE
The glint of the sequins can be blinding! Inspired by 1920s cabaret theater, this determinedly trendy place in the Village has nightly performances and a dance floor. Friday and Saturday feature festive drag shows, which, on a given night, may honor Tina Turner or Céline Dion. Look for the pink-haired drag queen on the retro marquee. *1115 rue Ste-Catherine est.* ☎ *514/525-7566. www.mado.qc.ca. Cover C$5–C$10. Métro: Beaudry. Map p 107.*

Casa del Popolo PLATEAU   Set in a scruffy storefront, Casa del Popolo serves vegetarian food, operates a laid-back bar, and has a post-age-stamp-size first-floor stage. It's the sister property to La Sala Rosa (below), across the street. *4873 bd. St-Laurent.* ☎ *514/284-3804. www.casadelpopolo.com. Cover C$6–C$15. Métro: Laurier. Map p 107.*

Club Balattou PLATEAU   This club on the Main is a top venue for African music and performers from the West Indies and Latin America. An infectious, sensual beat issues from it. *4372 bd. St-Laurent.* ☎ *514/845-5447. www.lucubrium.com/balattou. Cover C$5–C$20 Métro: Mont-Royal. Map p 107.*

Club Soda QUARTIER LATIN   This long-established rock club in a seedy part of the Quartier Latin remains one of the prime destinations for performers just below the star level—Queensryche, Mara Tremblay, and Pauly Shore have all come through recently. *1225 bd. St-Laurent.* ☎ *514/286-1010. www.clubsoda.ca. Tickets from C$22. Métro: St-Laurent. Map p 107.*

Hurley's Irish Pub DOWNTOWN
One of the few nightspots where you'll see college kids, middle-aged folks, and retirees sharing a pint.

Rainbows abound in The Village, and even mark the Beaudry Métro entrance.

La Sala Rosa provides an intimate performance space.

Everyone enjoys the live Celtic instrumentalists who perform nightly, usually starting around 9:30pm. *1225 rue Crescent.* ☎ *514/861-4111. www.hurleysirishpub.com. Métro: Guy-Concordia. Map p 108.*

★ **La Sala Rosa** PLATEAU The heart of the Montréal indie music scene. This is a medium-size venue that offers a full calendar of interesting rock, experimental, and jazz music. The ground floor Sala Rosa Restaurant has live flamenco music every Thursday with dancing and singing—reserve your spot a week or more in advance. *4848 bd. St-Laurent.* ☎ *514/284-0122. www.casadelpopolo.com. Cover C$6–C$15. Métro: Laurier. Map p 107.*

Le Divan Orange PLATEAU A hopping club with a good, hipster vibe. Bands and combos here include indie rock, jazz, country, and traditional North African. There are also events best described as performance art. *4234 bd. St-Laurent.* ☎ *514/840-9090. www.ledivanorange.org. Cover C$5–C$10. Métro: Mont-Royal. Map p 107.*

★ **Maison du Jazz** DOWNTOWN Sax and trumpet solos ring blissfully from the stage as jazz hounds sit back and sip martinis at this New Orleans–style jazz venue. Music is of the swinging mainstream variety, with occasional digressions into more esoteric forms. *2060 rue Aylmer.* ☎ *514/842-8656. www.houseofjazz.ca. Cover C$5. Métro: McGill. Map p 108.*

★ **Upstairs Jazz Bar & Grill** DOWNTOWN Big names are infrequent at the Upstairs bar (which you have to walk downstairs to enter), but the groups are more than competent. Sets begin as early as 7:30pm. Food ranges from bar snacks to more substantial meals. *1254 rue Mackay.* ☎ *514/931-6808. www.upstairsjazz.com. Cover C$5–C$30. Métro: Guy-Concordia. Map p 108.* ●

The legendary Maison du Jazz is still the best place in town for jazz aficionados.

A&E in Montréal

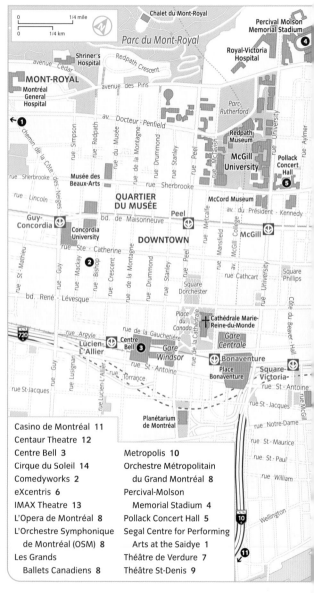

Casino de Montréal 11
Centaur Theatre 12
Centre Bell 3
Cirque du Soleil 14
Comedyworks 2
eXcentris 6
IMAX Theatre 13
L'Opera de Montréal 8
L'Orchestre Symphonique
  de Montréal (OSM) 8
Les Grands
  Ballets Canadiens 8

Metropolis 10
Orchestre Métropolitain
  du Grand Montréal 8
Percival-Molson
  Memorial Stadium 4
Pollack Concert Hall 5
Segal Centre for Performing
  Arts at the Saidye 1
Théâtre de Verdure 7
Théâtre St-Denis 9

Previous page: Montréal is home to the captivating Cirque du Soleil.

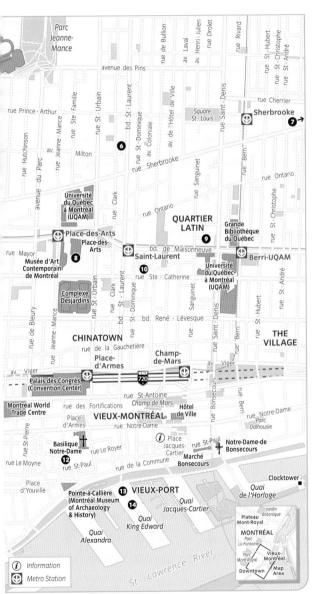

A&E Best Bets

La Centre Bell is home to many of the city's concerts and its beloved Canadiens.

Best Free Classical Music
Pollack Concert Hall, *555 rue Sherbrooke ouest (p 120)*

Best English-Speaking Theater
★ Centaur Theatre, *453 rue St-Francois-Xavier (p 121)*

Best Yiddish-Speaker Theater
Segal Centre for Performing Arts at the Saidye, *5170 Côte-Ste-Catherine (p 122)*

Best Circus
★★★ Cirque du Soleil *(p 119)*

Best Sports Venue
★ Centre Bell, *1260 rue de la Gauchetiere ouest (p 121)*

Best Concert Venue for Big-Name Bands
★ Centre Bell, *1260 rue de la Gauchetiere ouest (p 121)*

Best Refined Evening Entertainment
★★ L'Orchestre Symphonique de Montréal, *Place des Arts, 175 Ste-Catherine ouest (p 119)*

Best Free Entertainment
★ Théâtre Verdure, *Parc La Fontaine (p 122)*

Best Comedy Spot
Comedyworks, *1238 rue Bishop (p 120)*

Best Rock Concert Venue
Metropolis, *59 Ste-Catherine est (p 121)*

Best Last-Minute Ticket Deals
★ Vitrine Culturelle de Montréal, *145 rue Ste-Catherine ouest (Place des Arts; p 169)*

Best Humungous Movie Screen
IMAX Theatre, *in the Centre des Sciences de Montréal, Quai King Edward (p 120)*

Best Destination for Games of Chance
Casino de Montréal, *Parc Jean-Drapeau (p 119)*

Best Drag Club
Cabaret Mado, *1115 rue Ste-Catherine est (p 113)*

Best Small Venue for Indie Rock
★ La Sala Rosa, *4848 bd. St-Laurent (p 114)*

Best Old-Time Jazz & Dinner Club
★ Maison du Jazz, *2060 rue Aylmer (p 114)*

Best Bike Rentals
ÇaRoule/Montréal on Wheels, *27 rue de la Commune est (p 52)*

Montréal A&E A to Z

Casino

Casino de Montréal PARC JEAN-DRAPEAU The province's first casino is housed in a complex recycled from the French and Québec pavilions from the 1967 World's Fair, Expo 67. Asymmetrical and groovy, the buildings provide a dramatic setting for games of chance. Four floors contain more than 120 game tables, including roulette, craps, blackjack, baccarat, and varieties of poker. More than 3,200 slot machines create a mind-numbing din. Admission is restricted to persons 18 and over. *Parc Jean-Drapeau.* ☎ *800/665-2274 or 514/392-2746. www.casinosdu quebec.com. Free admission. Métro: Parc Jean-Drapeau. Map p 116.*

Circus

★★★ Cirque du Soleil A circus unlike any other, the internationally acclaimed Cirque du Soleil conjures up stunning performances that combine death-defying acrobatics, sensual choreography, ethereal music, and vivid stage sets. The troupe performs internationally, with as many as 19 shows simultaneously. Although Montréal is its home base, there isn't a permanent show here. Still, it often sets up its signature blue and yellow tents in Vieux-Port in late spring. *Expensive (tickets run C$55–C$130), but worth every penny. Tickets can be purchased at the Cirque website. www.cirquedusoleil.com. Map p 116.*

Classical Music

★★★ L'Opera de Montréal DOWNTOWN Wonderful performances of classics such as Mozart's *The Magic Flute* and Puccini's *Tosca* are surtitled in French and English, with video translations rarely interfering with the dazzling sets below.

The Casino de Montréal.

Heavily discounted tickets are sometimes available for final dress rehearsals. *Place des Arts, 175 Ste-Catherine ouest.* ☎ *514/985-2258. www.opera demontreal.com. Tickets from C$46. Métro: Place des Arts. Map p 116.*

★★ L'Orchestre Symphonique de Montréal (OSM) DOWNTOWN Kent Nagano was brought on as music director in 2005 and has focused this world-famous orchestra's repertoire on programs featuring works by Beethoven, Bach, Brahms, Mahler, and Messiaen. All is not staid: The orchestra performs at Place des Arts, occasionally at the Notre-Dame Basilica, and offers a few free concerts in parks each summer. *Place des Arts, 175 Ste-Catherine ouest.* ☎ *514/842-9951. www. osm.ca. Tickets from C$25, discounts available for people under 30. Métro: Place des Arts. Map p 116.*

Orchestre Métropolitain du Grand Montréal DOWNTOWN This orchestra performs during its regular season at Place des Arts. Its 2010 schedule includes Mahler's Symphony No. 8. In summer, the group presents free outdoor concerts at Théâtre de Verdure in Parc La Fontaine. *Place des Arts, 175 Ste-Catherine ouest.* ☎ *866/842-2112 or*

The Orchestre Métropolitain du Grand Montréal performs at Place des Arts and, in summer, at Théâtre de Verdure in Parc La Fontaine.

514/842-2112. www.orchestre metropolitain.com. *Tickets from C$25. Métro: Place des Arts. Map p 116.*

Pollack Concert Hall DOWN-TOWN   A stone statue of Queen Victoria perched on her throne guards the entrance to this 1908 landmark building on the McGill University campus, where many classical concerts and recitals are staged. Because most of the concerts are performed by McGill students or alumni, tickets are modest—in fact, most are free. *555 rue Sherbrooke ouest.* ☎ *514/398-4547. www.music. mcgill.ca. Tickets free–C$30. Métro: McGill. Map p 116.*

Comedy
Comedyworks DOWNTOWN This long-running club entertains patrons every day with improvisational groups and open-mic nights. The best nights to come are Thursday through Saturday, when better-known comedians take the stage. Sit in the back if you don't want to heckled by the performers. *1238 rue Bishop.* ☎ *514/398-9661. www.comedyworks montreal.com. Cover from C$5. Métro: Guy-Concordia. Map p 116.*

Dance
★★ Les Grands Ballets Canadiens DOWNTOWN   A breathtaking Christmas-season rendition of *The Nutcracker* is this internationally renowned ballet company's most popular event of the year. *Place des Arts, 175 Ste-Catherine ouest.* ☎ *514/ 842-2112. www.grandballets.qc.ca. Tickets from C$26. Métro: Place des Arts. Map p 116.*

Film
In Montréal, English-language films are usually presented with French subtitles. However, when the letters VF (for version française) follow the title of a non-Francophone movie, it means that the movie has been dubbed into French. Policies vary regarding English subtitles on non-English-language films, so ask at the box office. Movie admission is usually about C$10 for adults and less for seniors, students, and children. There are often special afternoon rates for matinees.

eXcentris PLATEAU   The Ex-Centris has long been a cutting-edge Plateau Mont-Royal independent film venue and began transitioning its programming in late 2009. The new iteration (redubbed eXcentris) promises to be an "iconic new media complex" that features "music, theater, poetry, visual arts and dance, in an ambiance of fine food and drink, seductive design, and seamless technology." *3530 bd. St-Laurent.* ☎ *514/ 847-2206. www.excentris.com. Métro: Sherbrooke. Map p 116.*

IMAX Theatre VIEUX-PORT Imposing, fantastically huge images confront viewers of the seven-story IMAX screen in the Centre des Sciences de Montréal (Montréal Science Center). Many of the films are suitable for the entire family. *Quai King Edward.* ☎ *877/496-4724 or 514/496-4724. www.montrealscience centre.com. Tickets from C$12 adults,*

C$11 seniors and children 13–17, C$9 children 4–12, free for children 3 and under. *Métro: Place d'Armes or Champ-de-Mars. Map p 116.*

Sports and Rock Venues
★ **Centre Bell** DOWNTOWN   A dazzling facility and Montréal's largest all-purpose entertainment venue. It allows for all sorts of different stage arrangements and sports configurations and is home to hockey's Montréal Canadiens. It also brings in rock and pop performers such as KISS and Beyoncé (tragically, not together). *1260 rue de la Gauchetiere ouest.* ☎ *800/663-6786 or 514/989-2841. www.centrebell.ca. Métro: Bonaventure. Map p 116.*

Métropolis DOWNTOWN   After starting life as a skating rink in 1884, the Métropolis is now a prime showplace for traveling rock groups. It recently hosted Beirut, Estelle, Kool and the Gang, and the "Ethnic Heroes of Comedy" tour. *59 Ste-Catherine est.* ☎ *514/844-3500. www.montreal metropolis.ca/metropolis. Métro: St-Laurent. Map p 116.*

Percival-Molson Memorial Stadium DOWNTOWN   During the

Attending a Canadiens game in the Bell Centre is an experience few will forget.

A production at the Centaur Theatre, Montréal's primary English-language theater.

Canadian Football League season, this stadium gets incredibly loud on Sunday thanks to the die-hard, chest-painting fans of the Montréal Alouettes (that's French for "larks") who blow incessantly into deafening plastic horns. The team's reputation has skyrocketed with locals in recent years, and tickets to games at this venerable stadium sell out quickly. *Top of rue University at McGill University campus.* ☎ *514/871-2255 for Alouettes ticket info. www. montrealalouettes.com. Tickets from C$25. Métro: McGill. Map p 116.*

Theater
★ **Centaur Theatre** VIEUX-MONTREAL   The city's principal English-language theater is housed in a former stock-exchange building from 1903. It presents a mix of classics, foreign adaptations, and works by Canadian playwrights. Its reputation for showcasing some of the city's finest productions makes it a hot spot for tourists, and tickets to major plays are often hard to come by. *453 rue St-Francois-Xavier.* ☎ *514/288-3161. www.centaur theatre.com. Tickets from C$33. Métro: Place d'Armes. Map p 116.*

Theatrical performances are staged in both Yiddish and English at the Segal Centre for Performing Arts at the Saidye.

Segal Centre for Performing Arts at the Saidye PLATEAU

From about 1900 to 1930, Yiddish was Montréal's third most-common language. That status has since been usurped by any number of languages, but its dominance lives on here, one of the few North American theaters that still presents plays in Yiddish. *5170 Côte-Ste-Catherine.* ☎ *514/739-7944. www.saidye bronfman.org. Tickets from C$35.*

The Théâtre St-Denis fills with laughter during the Just for Laughs comedy festival.

Métro: Côte-Ste-Catherine or Snowdon. Map p 116.

★ Théâtre de Verdure PARC LA FONTAINE

In summer, the outdoor amphitheater in Parc La Fontaine is one of the best places to enjoy a show or concert. Tango nights in July are especially popular. Everything is free: music, dance, and theater, often with well-known artists and performers. Many in the audience pack picnics. Performances are held from June to August; check with the tourism office (p 156) for days and times. *Parc La Fontaine.* ☎ *514/872-4041. Free admission. Métro: Sherbrooke. Map p 116.*

Théâtre St-Denis QUARTIER LATIN

Recently refurbished, this theater complex in the heart of the Latin Quarter hosts a variety of shows by the likes of Norah Jones and Alice Cooper, as well as segments of the Juste pour Rire (Just for Laughs) comedy festival in July. *1594 rue St-Denis.* ☎ *514/849-4211. www.theatrestdenis.com. Métro: Berri-UQAM. Map p 116.* ●

Hotel Best Bets

Best **Boutique Hotel**
★★★ Hôtel Le Germain $$$
2050 rue Mansfield (p 129)

Best **Romantic Hotel**
★★ Auberge du Vieux-Port $$$
97 rue de la Commune est (p 127)

Best **Business Traveler Hotel**
★★ Sofitel $$$ *1155 rue
Sherbrooke ouest (p 132)*

Best **New Chain Hotel**
★ Embassy Suites (Hilton) $$
208 St-Antoine ouest (p 128)

Best **Contemporary Hotel**
★★★ W Montréal $$$$ *901 rue
Square Victoria (p 132)*; and
★★ Loews Hôtel Vogue $$$ *1425
rue de la Montagne (p 131)*

Best **High Design Hotel**
★★ Hôtel Gault $$$ *449 rue
Ste-Hélène (p 129)*; and ★★ Hôtel
St-Paul $$$ *355 rue McGill (p 130)*

Best **Unassuming Hotel**
★★ Hôtel XIXe Siècle $$$
262 rue St-Jacques (p 130)

Best **Bed & Breakfast**
★ Auberge Les Passants du Sans
Soucy $$ *171 rue St-Paul ouest
(p 127)*

Best **In-House Dining Options**
★★ Place d'Armes Hôtel & Suites
$$$ *55 rue St-Jacques ouest
(p 132)*

Best **to Feel Like Royalty**
Hôtel Le St-James $$$$$ *355 rue
St-Jacques (p 129)*

Best **to Step Back to the
18th Century**
★ Hostellerie Pierre du Calvet $$$
405 rue Bonsecours (p 128)

Best **for Families**
Hôtel du Fort $$ *1390 rue du Fort
(p 129)*

Best **Cheap Bed**
McGill Residences $ *3425 rue
University (p 131)*

*A bedroom at the Auberge Les Passants du Sans Soucy, a quintessential Old
Montréal hotel.*

Previous page: A bedroom in the Hotel Place d'Armes.

Accommodations in Vieux-Montréal

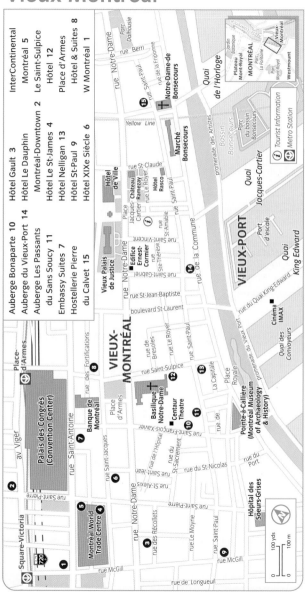

InterContinental Montréal 5
Le Saint-Sulpice Hôtel 12
Place d'Armes Hôtel & Suites 8
W Montréal 1

Hôtel Gault 3
Hôtel Le Dauphin Montréal-Downtown 2
Hôtel Le St-James 4
Hôtel Nelligan 13
Hôtel St-Paul 9
Hôtel XIXe Siècle 6

Auberge Bonaparte 10
Auberge du Vieux-Port 14
Auberge Les Passants du Sans Soucy 11
Embassy Suites 7
Hostellerie Pierre du Calvet 15

Accommodations in Downtown Montréal

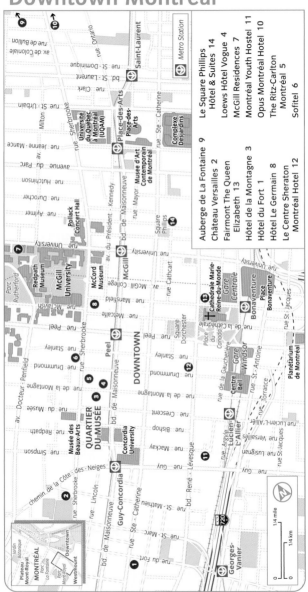

Auberge de La Fontaine 9
Château Versailles 2
Fairmont The Queen Elizabeth 13
Hôtel de la Montagne 3
Hôtel du Fort 1
Hôtel Le Germain 8
Le Centre Sheraton Montréal Hotel 12
Le Square Phillips Hôtel & Suites 14
Loews Hôtel Vogue 4
McGill Residences 7
Montréal Youth Hostel 11
Opus Montréal Hotel 10
The Ritz-Carlton Montréal 5
Sofitel 6

Hotels **A to Z**

★ **Auberge Bonaparte** VIEUX-
MONTREAL   Even the smallest
rooms in this fashionable urban inn
are sizeable, with comfortable beds
and bright decor. Generous breakfasts are included, and sitting at one
of the elegant window tables of restaurant Bonaparte with a newspaper,
a croissant, and an omelet is an especially civilized way to start the day.
447 rue St-François-Xavier. ☎ *514/844-
1448. www.bonaparte.com. 31 units.
Doubles C$170–C$215. AE, DC, MC, V.
Métro: Place d'Armes. Map p 125.*

★ **Auberge de La Fontaine**
PLATEAU   For visitors who plan to
spend time at the restaurants and
bars of Plateau Mont-Royal and want
a casual option, La Fontaine can't be
beat. It feels like a cheerful hostel:
Breakfast tables fill the lobby, a
kitchen with free snacks is available
from noon to midnight, and it's
located directly on the lovely Parc La
Fontaine and one of the city's central
bike paths. Bedrooms are done up in
bright, funky colors. *1301 rue Rachel
est.* ☎ *514/597-0166. www.auberge
delafontaine.com. 21 units. Doubles
C$153–C$193. AE, DC, MC, V. Métro:
Mont-Royal. Map p 126.*

★★ **Auberge du Vieux-Port**
VIEUX-MONTREAL   Terrifically
romantic. This luxury inn in an 1882
building faces the waterfront, and
many rooms as well as a rooftop terrace offer unobstructed views of
Vieux-Port, a particular treat on summer nights when there are fireworks
on the river. In addition to modern
comforts, you'll find stone walls and
wooden beams. *97 rue de la Commune est.* ☎ *888/660-7678 or 514/876-
0081. www.aubergeduvieuxport.com.
27 units. Doubles C$179–C$285. AE,
DC, MC, V. Métro: Champ-de-
Mars. Map p 125.*

*Start the day in style with a light break-
fast at restaurant Bonaparte.*

★ **Auberge Les Passants du
Sans Soucy** VIEUX-MONTREAL
One of the first places to consider
when staying in Vieux-Montréal.
Captivating rooms have rustic
touches such as exposed brick,
wood-beamed ceilings, and small
fireplaces. Substantial morning meals
include chocolate croissants and
made-to-order omelets. *171 rue St-
Paul ouest.* ☎ *514/842-2634. www.
lesanssoucy.com. 9 units. Doubles
C$160–C$190. AE, MC, V. Métro:
Place d'Armes. Map p 125.*

Bed & Breakfasts

B&Bs boast cozy settings and are
often (but not always) less expensive
than comparable hotels. They also
give visitors an opportunity to meet
a Montréaler or two. The Association
des Gîtes Touristiques de Montréal
(the Bed & Breakfast Association of
Montréal) lists B&Bs and guesthouses that are approved by the
province's tourist board. *You can
call the board at* ☎ *514/510-7976 or
visit its website, www.agtm.ca. You
can also find B&Bs at www.tourisme-
montreal.org.*

A deluxe room at the atmospheric Château Versailles.

★ **Château Versailles** DOWN-TOWN   Official lodging of the Musée des Beaux-Arts, the Versailles is near the museum but outside most of the tourist orbit. Its amiable staff will lug your baggage up the stairs of the elevator-free pre–World War I building. *1659 rue Sherbrooke ouest.* ☎ *888/ 933-8111 or 514/933-8111. www. versailleshotels.com. 65 units. Doubles C$169–C$220. AE, DC, DISC, MC, V. Métro: Guy-Concordia. Map p 126.*

★ **Embassy Suites** VIEUX-MON-TREAL   This new hotel from the Hilton empire is part of an expanding hotel row opposite the Palais des Congrès (Convention Center). Most units are bona fide suites with pull-out sofas, big-screen TVs, and kitchens with microwaves and fridges, making it particularly welcoming for families and road warriors. Cooked-to-order breakfasts and an evening cocktail are included in the room rate, which can add up to a significant savings. *208 St-Antoine ouest.* ☎ *514/288-8886. www.embassy suitesmontreal.com. 210 units. Doubles C$204–C$280. AE, DC, DISC, MC, V. Métro: Place d'Armes. Map p 125.*

★★ **kids Fairmont The Queen Elizabeth** DOWNTOWN   The city's largest and most convenient hotel sits atop the main train station, with the Métro and popular shopping areas accessible through underground arcades. The "Queen E" goes to great lengths when it comes to guests' comfort and is a frequent choice for heads of state and touring celebrities. *900 bd. René-Lévesque ouest.* ☎ *866/540-4483 or 514/861-3511. www.fairmont.com. 1,039 units. Doubles C$189–C$359. AE, DC, MC, V. Métro: Bonaventure. Map p 126.*

★ **Hostellerie Pierre du Calvet** VIEUX-MONTREAL   Step from cobblestone streets into an opulent 18th-century home boasting gold-leafed writing desks and four-poster beds of teak mahogany. Some bedrooms have fireplaces, and room no. 6 even has a shower with stone walls. In warm months, an outdoor courtyard with a small fountain is a hideaway dining terrace. *405 rue Bonsecours.* ☎ *866/544-1725 or 514/282-1725. www.pierreducalvet.ca. 10 units. Doubles C$265–C$295. AE, MC, V. Métro: Champ-de-Mars. Map p 125.*

Hôtel de la Montagne DOWN-TOWN   The gilded fairy with stained-glass wings presents a grand impression in the lobby. Room furnishings seem bland by comparison, though some of the more expensive rooms have gotten a sleek update in recent years. All units have good-size bathrooms and high-end bedding.

The bedrooms at the historic Fairmont The Queen Elizabeth are some of the most luxurious in town.

other hand, bathrooms are sleek with glass-walled shower stalls, beds are comfy, and—get this—all units are equipped with a computer terminal and free Internet access. The location, on the northern end of Vieux-Montréal, is central, though the immediate surroundings are nondescript. *1025 rue de Bleury.* ☎ *888/784-3888 or 514/788-3888. www.hotelsdauphin.ca. 72 units. Doubles C$129–C$159. AE, MC, V. Métro Place d'Armes. Map p 125.*

★★★ **Hôtel Le Germain** DOWNTOWN The vibe here is stylish loft, mixing Asian minimalism with Western comforts. Bedrooms have super-comfy bedding, marshmallowy-plush reading chairs, ergonomic work areas with eye-level plugs, and a glass partition between the bed and the shower. There's free espresso in the lobby. *2050 rue Mansfield.* ☎ *877/333-2050 or 514/849-2050. www.hotelgermain.com. 101 units. Doubles C$210–C$475. AE, DC, MC, V. Métro: Peel. Map p 126.*

★★★ **Hôtel Le St-James** VIEUX-MONTREAL Gorgeous and elegant. The grand hall houses the hotel's ornate XO Le Restaurant, and sumptuous bedrooms are furnished with entrancing antiques and impeccable

The outdoor terrace at the Hostellerie Pierre du Calvet is lovely in warm weather.

1430 rue de la Montagne. ☎ *800/361-6262 or 514/288-5656. www.hoteldelamontagne.com. 142 units. Doubles C$175–C$249. AE, DC, DISC, MC, V. Métro: Peel. Map p 126.*

kids Hôtel du Fort DOWNTOWN This reliable hotel takes as its primary duty providing lodging to longer-term business travelers and families. There are basic kitchenettes with fridges and microwave ovens in every unit, and many have sofa beds. *1390 rue du Fort.* ☎ *800/565-6333 or 514/938-8333. www.hoteldufort.com. 124 units. Doubles C$179–C$225. AE, DC, MC, V. Métro: Guy-Concordia. Map p 126.*

★★ **Hôtel Gault** VIEUX-MONTREAL Gault explores the far reaches of minimalism, and design aficionados will likely love it. With raw, monumental concrete walls, its structural austerity is stark but tempered by lollipop-colored reproductions of mod furniture from the 1950s. Large bedrooms are loft style and employ curtains instead of walls to define spaces. *449 rue Ste-Hélène.* ☎ *866/904-1616 or 514/904-1616. www.hotelgault.com. 30 units. Doubles C$220–C$389. AE, MC, V. Métro: Square Victoria. Map p 125.*

Hôtel Le Dauphin Montréal-Downtown VIEUX-MONTREAL Room furnishings are simple if somewhat dorm-room functional. On the

Hôtel Gault's minimalist style and mod furniture mix sleek style and colorful whimsy.

reproductions. A member of the exclusive Leading Small Hotels of the World, Le St-James represents a triumph of design and preservation for visiting royalty—and those who want to be treated like it. *355 rue St-Jacques.* ☎ *866/841-3111 or 514/841-3111. www.hotellestjames.com. 61 units. Doubles C$425–C$475. AE, DC, DISC, MC, V. Métro: Square Victoria. Map p 125.*

★ **Hôtel Nelligan** VIEUX-MONTREAL   Many of the Nelligan's bedrooms are dark-wooded, masculine retreats, with heaps of pillows and quality mattresses. You can dine at the ground floor Verses restaurant or on the rooftop terrace in warm months, where drinks and light meals are served until 11pm. *106 rue St-Paul ouest.* ☎ *877/788-2040 or 514/788-2040. www.hotelnelligan. com. 105 units. Doubles C$235–C$260. AE, DC, DISC, MC, V. Métro: Place d'Armes. Map p 125.*

★★ **Hôtel St-Paul** VIEUX-MONTREAL   The chic St-Paul has been a star to design and architecture aficionados since its 2001 opening. Minimalism pervades, with simple lines

The all-suite Le Saint-Sulpice is a great option for families looking for extra room.

and muted colors. This being Canada, pops of texture come from pelt rugs. Many rooms face Vieux-Montréal's less-touristed far-western edge, with its mixture of stone and brick buildings. *355 rue McGill.* ☎ *866/380-2202 or 514/380-2222. www.hotelstpaul. com. 120 units. Doubles C$223–C$279. AE, MC, V. Métro: Square Victoria. Map p 125.*

★★ **Hôtel XIXe Siècle** VIEUX-MONTREAL   This tidy little hotel is worth seeking out for its central location, superior service, and spacious rooms, which feature 4.5m (15-ft.) ceilings, large windows, and functional work desks. The Second Empire interiors reflect its 1870 origins as a bank. *262 rue St-Jacques.* ☎ *877/553-0019 or 514/985-0019. www.hotelxixsiecle.com. 59 units. Doubles C$185–C$220. AE, DC, MC, V. Métro: Place d'Armes. Map p 125.*

★ **InterContinental Montréal** VIEUX-MONTREAL   Open since 1991, this hotel started a floor-to-ceiling renovation in 2008 of its rooms, lobby, bar, restaurant, and reception area. New guest rooms are spacious, well lit, and, in many cases, romantic. *360 rue St-Antoine ouest.* ☎ *800/361-3600 or 514/987-9900. www.montreal.intercontinental.com. 357 units. Doubles C$212–C$259. AE, DC, DISC, MC, V. Métro: Square Victoria. Map p 125.*

★ **Le Centre Sheraton Montréal Hotel** DOWNTOWN   A modern business hotel that caters primarily to the suit-and-tie crowd. The central location, good-size rooms, and amenities including a pool and fitness center with skylights make it a good choice for leisure travelers, too. *1201 bd. René-Lévesque ouest.* ☎ *800/325-3535 or 514/878-2000. www.sheraton.com/lecentre. 825 units. Doubles C$189–C$599. AE, DC, DISC, MC, V. Métro: Bonaventure. Map p 126.*

★★ kids Le Saint-Sulpice Hôtel

VIEUX-MONTREAL This elite all-suite hotel is a great choice for the families who can afford its high price tag. In-room features include a mini-kitchen, separate seating areas, multiple TVs, and, in many of the suites, fireplaces or balconies. *414 rue St-Sulpice. ☎ 877/785-7423 or 514/288-1000. www.lesaintsulpice.com. 108 units. Doubles C$429–C$474. AE, DC, DISC, MC, V. Métro: Place d'Armes. Map p 125.*

★ Le Square Phillips Hôtel & Suites

DOWNTOWN Vaguely cathedral-like spaces make for capacious studio bedrooms and suites fully equipped for long stays. Full kitchens in every unit come with all the essential appliances, and there's a laundry room available. There's also an exercise room and a rooftop pool with a lovely view. *1193 Square Phillips. ☎ 866/393-1193 or 514/393-1193. www.squarephillips.com. 160 units. Doubles C$179–C$199. AE, DC, DISC, MC, V. Métro: McGill. Map p 126.*

★★ kids Loews Hôtel Vogue

DOWNTOWN Confidence and capability resonate from every member of the Loews staff, and luxury permeates from the lobby to the well-appointed guest rooms. Feather pillows and duvets dress oversize beds, and huge marble bathrooms are fitted with Jacuzzis. The hotel's L'Opéra Bar is a two-story room with floor-to-ceiling windows, and is open until 2am. *1425 rue de la Montagne. ☎ 888/465-6654 or 514/285-5555. www.loewshotels.com. 142 units. Doubles C$229–C$329. AE, DC, DISC, MC, V. Métro: Peel. Map p 126.*

McGill Residences

DOWNTOWN From mid-May to mid-August, McGill University opens its residence halls to travelers. The newest dorm is a converted Renaissance-Montreal hotel which offers hotel-like units with two beds and a private bathroom. Other halls have single rooms and shared

The dining room at the top notch Loews Hôtel Vogue.

baths. *3425 rue University. ☎ 514/398-5200. www.mcgill.ca/residences/summer. Singles C$45. MC, V. Métro: McGill. Map p 126.*

Montréal Youth Hostel

DOWNTOWN Dude! Rue Crescent and all the bars that stay open 'til 3am? They're only 2 blocks away! We are so totally set! *1030 rue Mackay. ☎ 866/843-3317 or 514/843-3317. www.hostellingmontreal.com. 240 beds. Single bed C$31, private room C$86. Free for children 5 and under. AE, DC, MC, V. Métro: Lucien-L'Allier. Map p 126.*

★ Opus Montréal Hotel

DOWNTOWN One of Montréal's nightlife epicenters is Opus's restaurant and bar, Koko (p 111), which boasts the city's most expansive terrace. Hotel guests can cut its notoriously long lines and sip neon drinks among the clubbing elite. Bedrooms are designed for this crowd, with showers that are lit from below, silky soft linens, and bedside earplugs. *10 rue Sherbrooke ouest. ☎ 866/744-6346 or 514/843-6000. www.opushotel.com. 136 units. Doubles C$229–C$249. AE, DC, DISC, MC, V. Métro: St-Laurent. Map p 126.*

The marble bathrooms at Place d'Armes Hôtel & Suites have such first-rate amenities as flatscreen TVs and separate showers.

★★ Place d'Armes Hôtel & Suites VIEUX-MONTREAL

One of the top romantic hotels in Montréal. Many bedrooms have high ceilings and original brick walls, and all feature contemporary deluxe bedding, slate floors in the bathrooms, and spotlight lighting. There are two terrific in-house dining options: the high-end Aix Cuisine du Terroir (p 98), and the visually arresting Suite 701 bar. *55 rue St-Jacques ouest.* ☎ *888/450-1887 or 514/842-1887. www.hotelplacedarmes.com. 135 units. Doubles C$225–C$285. AE, DC, DISC, MC, V. Métro: Place d'Armes. Map p 125.*

The Ritz-Carlton Montréal

DOWNTOWN   The Ritz and its restaurants have been closed for renovations and are expected to reopen in November 2010. Since its launch in 1912, the luxe hotel has been a favorite for both accommodations and dining, with Café de Paris favored for high tea and Le Jardin du Ritz for its duck pond and ducklings. Check the website for updates and pricing details. *1228 rue Sherbrooke ouest.* ☎ *800/363-0366 or 514/842-4212.*

www.ritzmontreal.com. Métro: Peel. Map p 126.

★★ Sofitel DOWNTOWN

The 100 standard rooms (called "superior") have floor-to-ceiling windows, furnishings made from Québec-grown cherrywood, down duvets, and soothing oatmeal-cream decor. Catering to the international and business guests whose bodies are operating on different time zones, its exercise room is open round-the-clock. *1155 rue Sherbrooke ouest.* ☎ *514/285-9000. www.sofitel.com. 258 units. Doubles C$215–C$290. AE, DC, MC, V. Métro: Peel. Map p 126.*

★★★ W Montréal VIEUX-MONTREAL

The brazen W serves up a nightclub atmosphere. It's also home to the intimate W Café/Bartini, which concocts specialty martinis and is often open until 3am, and the Wunderbar, which picks up the pace with beat-spinning DJs, also until 3am. Plush, high-tech bedrooms are designed with bathrooms that offer little privacy. *901 rue Square Victoria.* ☎ *877/946-8357 or 514/395-3100. www.whotels.com/montreal. 152 units. Doubles C$259–C$729. AE, DC, DISC, MC, V. Métro: Square Victoria. Map p 125.* ●

The high-tech rooms at the W Montréal are some of the plushest in town.

Québec City

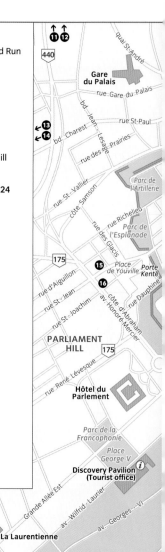

1. Château Frontenac
2. Terrasse Dufferin and the Bobsled Run
3. La Citadelle
4. Parc des Champs-de-Bataille
5. Aux Anciens Canadiens
6. Rue du Trésor
7. Funicular
8. Rue du Petit-Champlain
9. Musée de la Civilisation
10. Cirque du Soleil and the Image Mill

Where to Stay

Auberge Internationale de Québec 24
Auberge Le Vincent 13
Auberge Place d'Armes 26
Auberge Saint-Antoine 23
Cap Diamant 29
Courtyard Marriott Québec 16
Dominion 1912 20
Fairmont Le Château Frontenac 28
Hôtel Champlain Vieux-Québec 25
Hôtel de Glace 11
Hôtel-Musée Premières Nations 12

Where to Dine

Aux Anciens Canadiens 27
Laurie Raphaël 18
Le Café du Monde 21
Le Clocher Penché Bistrot 14
L'Echaudé 19
Le Pain Béni 26
Mistral Gagnant 17
Panache 23
Ristorante Il Teatro 15
Toast! 22

Previous page: Skiers riding to the top of Mont-Tremblant.

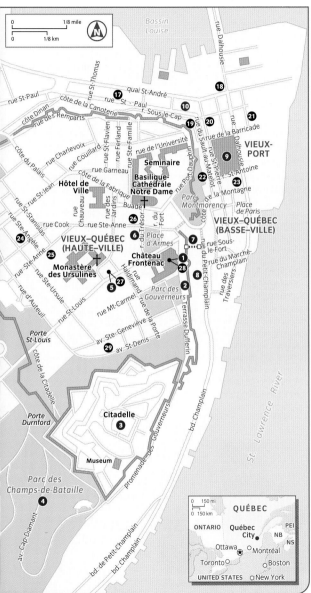

0 | 1/8 mile
0 | 1/8 km

Bassin Louise

rue Dalhousie

rue St-Paul
côte Dinan
rue des Remparts
côte de la Canoterie
rue St-Thomas
quai St-André
rue St - Paul
r. Sous-le-Cap

17
18
10
19
20
21

rue Charlevoix
côte du Palais
rue Couillard
rue St-Flavien
rue Ferland
rue Ste-Famille
rue de l'Université
rue du Sault-au-Matelot
rue St-Pierre
rue de la Barricade
rue Dalhousie

VIEUX-PORT

9
22
23

rue St-Antoine

rue Garneau
côte de la Fabrique
Seminaire
Basilique-Cathédrale Notre Dame

Hôtel de Ville
côte de la Fabrique
rue des Jardins
rue Chauveau
Buade
rue du Trésor
r. du Fort

Parc Montmorency

côte de la Montagne
Place de Paris

VIEUX-QUÉBEC (BASSE-VILLE)

rue Ste-Anne
rue Cook
rue St-Jean
rue St-Stanislas
rue Ste-Angèle

24
26
6
Place d'Armes

VIEUX-QUÉBEC (HAUTE-VILLE)

25
Monastère des Ursulines

rue Ste-Ursule
rue Ste-Anne
rue d'Auteuil
rue St-Louis

27
5

Château Frontenac
rue Haldimand

1
28
2
8

rue Sous-le-Fort
rue du Petit-Champlain
rue du Marché-Champlain
rue des Traversiers

Parc des Gouverneurs

rue Mt-Carmel
rue de la Porte
Porte St-Louis
av-Ste-Geneviève
av-St-Denis

29

côte de la Citadelle
Terrasse Dufferin

Porte Durnford

Citadelle

3

Museum

promenade des Gouverneurs
bd. Champlain

St. Lawrence River

Parc des Champs-de-Bataille

4

av-Cap-Diamant
bd. de Petit-Champlain
bd. Champlain

0 | 150 mi
0 | 150 km

QUÉBEC

ONTARIO | Québec City | PEI
| | NB
| | NS
Ottawa | Montréal
Toronto | Boston
UNITED STATES | New York

Québec City seduces from first view. Situated along the majestic Fleuve Saint-Laurent (St. Lawrence River), much of the oldest part of the city—Vieux-Québec, or, in English, Old Québec—sits atop Cap Diamant, a rock bluff that once provided military defense. Fortress walls still encase the upper city, and the soaring Château Frontenac, a hotel with castlelike turrets, dominates the landscape. A revitalized Lower Town, by the water, is thick with boutique hotels and cafes. The city is almost entirely French in feeling, spirit, and language: Almost everyone—95% of the population—is Francophone, or French speaking. But many of the 632,000 residents do know some English, especially those who work in hotels, restaurants, and shops.

START: **A full day stroll can take in the sites below in the order presented. Start at Place d'Armes, the central plaza in the upper city.**

❶ ★★★ **Château Frontenac.** The original section of the famous edifice that defines the Québec City skyline was built as a hotel from 1892 to 1893 by the Canadian Pacific Railway Co. The architect, an American named Bruce Price, raised his creation on the site of the governor's mansion and named it after Louis de Buade, comte de Frontenac, an early governor general of New France. Guided tours are available. See p 141 for information about staying here. *1 rue des Carrières.* ☎ *418/691-2166. www.tours chateau.ca. Tours C$8.50 adults, C$8 seniors, C$6 children 6–16, free for children 5 and under. May 1–Oct 15 daily 10am–6pm; Oct 16–Apr 30 Sat–Sun noon–5pm. Departures on the hour.*

The striking Château Frontenac is the most photographed hotel in the world.

❷ ★ **kids** **Terrasse Dufferin and the bobsled run.** In the warm months, this boardwalk promenade, with its green-and-white-topped gazebos, looks much as it did 100 years ago, when ladies with parasols and gentlemen with top hats and canes strolled along it on sunny afternoons. The terrace offers vistas of river, watercraft, and distant mountains, and is particularly romantic at sunset. Recent maintenance work underneath the promenade turned up remnants of forts and other buildings dating back to 1620, and visitors can now walk through the excavation site on self-directed tours. In winter, an old-fashioned toboggan run called Les Glissades de la Terrasse is set up on the steep wooden staircase on the south end, with the slide extending almost to the château. A little sugar shack is also set up in winter to sell sweet treats. *Bobsled information:* ☎ *418/829-9898. Cost is C$2 per person.*

❸ ★★ **kids** **La Citadelle.** The duke of Wellington had this partially star-shaped fortress built at the south end of the city walls in anticipation of American attacks after the War of 1812 (attacks that never came). The facility has never actually exchanged fire with an invader but continues its vigil for the state. It's

The long staircase running from La Citadelle to Terrace Dufferin is converted into a bobsled run during Québec City's winter carnival.

now a national historic site, and since 1920 has been home to Québec's Royal 22e Régiment, the only fully Francophone unit in Canada's armed forces. That makes it North America's largest fortified group of buildings still occupied by troops. Entrance is by guided tour only. If you're inclined, try to time a visit to include the ceremonies of the changing of the guard (daily at 10am July 24–Sept 6) or beating the retreat, a sunset ceremony to call in the troops (Fri and Sat at 7pm July–Aug). *Côte de la Citadelle.* ☎ *418/694-2815. www.lacitadelle.qc.ca. Admission C$10 adults, C$9 seniors and students, C$5.50 children 17 and under.*

June 24–Sept 6 daily 9am–6pm, shorter hours rest of the year. May be canceled in the event of rain.

④ ★★ kids Parc des Champs-de-Bataille. Covering 108 hectares (267 acres) of grassy hills, sunken gardens, monuments, fountains, and trees, Québec's Battlefields Park was Canada's first national urban park. A section called the Plains of Abraham is where Britain's general James Wolfe and France's Louis-Joseph, marquis de Montcalm, engaged in their short but crucial battle in 1759 which resulted in the British defeat of France. It also was the site of huge concerts by Céline Dion and Paul McCartney in 2008 for the city's 400th anniversary celebrations (videos of both shows are on YouTube). The park is a favorite place for Québécois when they want sunshine or a bit of exercise during all seasons of the year. *www.ccbn-nbc.gc.ca.*

Try Québécois home cooking right at **⑤ ★ Aux Anciens Canadiens,** a venerable restaurant with costumed servers is in what's probably the city's oldest (1677) house. Prices are generally high but the restaurant's afternoon table d'hôte special, from noon to 5:45pm, is a terrific bargain: soup, a main course, a dessert, and a glass of beer or wine for C$20.

Québec City 101

High season in Québec City is from June 24 (Jean-Baptiste Day) through Labour Day (the first Mon in Sept, as in the U.S.). Almost all of a visit can be spent on foot in the old Upper Town, atop Cap Diamant (Cape Diamond), and in the old Lower Town, which hugs the river below the bluff. There's a central tourist information center in Upper Town on Place d'Armes. Centre Infotouriste de Québec (12 rue Ste-Anne; ☎ 877/266-5687; www.bonjourquebec.com) is run by Québec province's tourism department and is open from 8:30am to 8:30pm daily. The city's own tourism website is www.quebecregion.com.

Aux Anciens Canadiens is charming inside and out.

Consider caribou in blueberry-wine sauce or Québéc meat pie, and don't pass up the maple sugar pie with cream. *See p 142.*

6 Rue du Trésor. Artists hang their prints and paintings of Québec scenes on both sides of this narrow pedestrian lane. In decent weather, it's busy with browsers and sellers. Most prices are within the means of the average visitor.

7 ★ kids Funicular. To get from Upper Town to Lower Town, you can take streets, staircases, or this cliffside elevator, known as the funicular. It operates along an inclined 64m

Watercolors, prints, and drawings can be purchased along Rue du Trésor.

(210-ft.) track and offers excellent aerial views during its short trip. The upper station is on Place d'Armes. It operates daily 7:30am until 11pm (until midnight in high season). Wheelchairs and strollers can be accommodated. The one-way fare is C$1.75. www.funiculaire-quebec.com.

8 ★ kids Rue du Petit-Champlain. This tiny, pedestrian-only shopping street is allegedly North America's oldest lane. It swarms with cafe sitters, strolling couples, and gaggles of schoolchildren in the warm months. In winter, it's a snowy wonderland with ice statues and twinkling white lights. If you're hungry, Le Lapin Saute (52 rue du Petit-Champlain; ☎ 418/692-5325), is a country-cozy bistro that has hearty food in generous portions and a lovely terrace overlooking a small garden. *www.quartierpetit champlain.com.*

9 ★★★ kids Musée de la Civilisation. This wonderful museum, which opened in 1988, may be housed in a lackluster gray-block building, but there is nothing plain about it once you enter. Spacious and airy, it has ingeniously arranged multidimensional exhibits. If time is short, definitely take in People of Québec Then and Now, a permanent exhibit that is a sprawling examination of Québec history, from the province's roots as a fur-trading colony to the turbulent movement for independence that started in the 1960s. *85 rue Dalhousie. ☎ 418/643-2158. www.mcq.org. Admission C$11 adults, C$10 seniors, C$8 students 17 and over, C$4 children 12–16, free for children 11 and under; free for all on Tues Nov 1–May 31 and Sat 10am–noon Jan–Feb. Late June to early Sept daily 9:30am–6:30pm, rest of the year Tues–Sun 10am–5pm.*

10 ★★ kids Cirque du Soleil and *The Image Mill*. There are two terrifically innovative events to plan summer evenings around: Through 2013, Cirque du Soleil will be performing on city streets every weekday evening from June 24 to Labour Day. Spectators will meet up with bands of circus performers at designated spots and then travel the streets with the troupes. Later at night, the 40-minute show *The Image Mill* will be projected in Vieux-Port along the massive wall of Bunge grain silos. A highlight of the 400th anniversary celebrations in 2008, the show will be presented Wednesday through Sunday. And the price is right: Both events are free! Details about both programs are on the city's website, www.quebecregion. com. For a taste of *The Image Mill*, see photos at www.lacaserne.net.

The Funiculaire offers wonderful views and allows you to skip the climb up the Breakneck Stairs.

Québec City: **Where to Stay**

kids Auberge Internationale de Québec There are 279 beds in this centrally located youth hostel, the largest in Canada. Most are in the dorm layouts standard to Hostelling International, while others are in modest private rooms for one to five people, with either shared or private bathrooms. *19 rue Ste-Ursule.* ☎ *866/694-0950 or 418/694-0755.*

A room at the refined Auberge Le Vincent.

www.aubergeinternationaldequebec. com. 279 beds (includes 23 private rooms). Private room for two C\$74–C\$87. AE, MC, V.

★ **Auberge Le Vincent**
Nestled in the emerging St-Roch neighborhood of tech companies, skateboard punks, and well-heeled hipsters are restaurants worth going out of your way for and the van Gogh–inspired Le Vincent. The sophisticated accommodations represent a terrific value. *295 rue St-Vallier est.* ☎ *888/523-5005 or 418/523-5000. www.aubergele vincent.com. 10 units. Doubles C\$199–C\$229 w/breakfast. AE, MC, V.*

★ **Auberge Place d'Armes**
Renovated in 2008, this high-end *auberge* offers 21 sumptuous rooms with stone walls that date from 1640 and handmade artisanal furniture—at surprisingly moderate prices. The *auberge* swallowed up a museum that had been here previously, and the most eye-popping

Value Meals, Québec Style

When dining out, always look for a table d'hôte option. These are fixed-price menus with three or four courses, and they usually cost little more than the price of a single a la carte main course. Restaurants at all price ranges offer them, and they present the best way to try out gourmet food for moderate prices. When offered at lunch, they are even less expensive.

unit, the Marie Antoinette suite, has actual 17th-century decor from Versailles. *24 rue Ste-Anne.* ☎ *866/333-9485 or 418/694-9485. www.auberge placedarmes.com. 21 units. Doubles C$150–C$200 w/breakfast. AE, MC, V.*

★★★ Auberge Saint-Antoine

This uncommonly attractive property began life as an 1830 maritime warehouse and kept the soaring ceilings, dark beams, and stone floors. It's now one of the city's landmark luxury boutique hotels and a member of the prestigious Relais & Chateaux luxury group. *8 rue St-Antoine.* ☎ *888/692-2211 or 418/692-2211. www.saint-antoine. com. 95 units. Doubles C$169–C$399 w/breakfast. AE, DC, MC, V.*

The striking and elegant Auberge Saint-Antoine.

Cap Diamant There are a lot of B&Bs in the pretty neighborhood behind the Château Frontenac. Owner Florence Guillot has turned this 1826 home into a grand Victoriana showpiece, with antiques and old photos richly decorating common areas and bedrooms. All rooms have private baths. *39 av. Ste-Geneviève.* ☎ *888/694-0303 or 418/694-0303. www.hotelcapdiamant.com. 9 units. Doubles C$164–C$174 w/breakfast. AE, MC, V.*

★★ [kids] Courtyard Marriott Québec

A hot property in recent years. It gets consistent raves on online boards for its friendly staff, comfortable rooms, and fair prices. It has also been named tops in staff service among all Courtyard hotels for 5 straight years. *850 Place d'Youville.* ☎ *866/694-4004 or 418/694-4004. www.marriott.com. 111 units. Doubles C$160–C$299. AE, DC, MC, V.*

★★★ Dominion 1912

Old Québec meets new in one of the city's most romantic boutique hotels. Québec-made beds are topped with mattresses that are deep, soft, and enveloping, heaped with pillows and feather duvets. A hearty continental breakfast is set out along with morning newspapers near the fireplace in the handsome lobby. *126 rue St-Pierre.* ☎ *888/833-5253 or 418/692-2224. www.hoteldominion.com. 60 units. Doubles C$169–C$425 w/breakfast. AE, DC, MC, V.*

Dominion 1912 blends Old Québec charm with modern amenities.

★★★ kids Fairmont Le Château Frontenac

Québec's magical "castle" opened in 1893 and has been wowing guests ever since. Many rooms are full-on luxurious, outfitted with elegant château furnishings and marble bathrooms. More than 500 (of 618) units were renovated in a 3-year project that finished in 2008. Prices depend on size, location, and view, with river views garnering top dollar. Lower-priced rooms overlooking the inner courtyard face gabled roofs, and children might imagine Harry Potter swooping by in a Quidditch match. *1 rue des Carrières.* ☎ *866/540-4460 or 418/692-3861. www.fairmont. com/frontenac. 618 units. Doubles C$259–C$499. AE, DC, DISC, MC, V.*

★ Hôtel Champlain Vieux-Québec

Even the smallest rooms in this recently renovated hotel have silk curtains, king or queen beds, 300-count cotton sheets, and flatscreen TVs. Most units are quite roomy. A self-serve espresso machine by the front desk provides free cappuccinos any time of day. *115 rue Ste-Anne.* ☎ *800/567-2106 or 418/694-0106. www.champlain hotel.com. 50 units. Doubles C$179–C$209 w/breakfast. AE, DISC, MC, V.*

Hôtel de Glace

Crafted each year from 500 tons of ice, Québec's ice hotel is built each winter at a woodsy resort a half-hour outside of the city. You can visit by day for C$16 or take one of the rooms from 9pm until 8am, before the next day's visitors arrive. It's open January through March. *Station touristique Duchesnay.* ☎ *877/505-0423. www. icehotel-canada.com. 36 units. Basic overnight package with dinner, breakfast, and cocktail from C$699 for two. AE, MC, V.*

★ Hôtel-Musée Premières Nations

Fifteen minutes from Québec City is a First Nations reservation called Wendake, and it's here that this beautifully airy, earthy hotel opened in early 2008. It's tucked into a grove of maple trees along the shores of the Akiawenrahk River and each room has a small balcony overlooking the river. *5 Place de la Rencontre, Wendake.* ☎ *866/551-9222 or 418/847-2222. www.hotelpremieres nations.ca. 55 units. Doubles C$149–C$179. AE, MC, V.*

Fairmont Le Château Frontenac is magical when lit up at night.

Québec City: **Where to Dine**

★ **Aux Anciens Canadiens** *TRADITIONAL QUEBECOIS* One of the best places in La Belle Province at which to sample cooking that has its roots in New France's earliest years. Québec's favorite dessert, sugar pie, reaches its apogee at this admittedly tourist-heavy venue in central Upper Town. Think maple syrup with a crust, or pecan pie without the pecans. *34 rue St-Louis.* ☎ *418/692-1627. www.aux ancienscanadiens.qc.ca. Entrees C$29–C$68. AE, DC, MC, V. Lunch & dinner daily.*

★★★ **Laurie Raphaël** *CONTEMPO-RARY QUEBECOIS* This smashingly creative restaurant tinkers relentlessly with its handiwork, building Willy Wonka–style concoctions. Silky-smooth foie gras arrives on a tiny ice cream paddle, drizzled with a port-and-maple-syrup reduction; an egg-yolk "illusion" of thickened orange juice encapsulated in a pectin skin is served in a puddle of maple syrup in

One of the many artistically presented dishes at Laurie Raphaël.

an Asian soup spoon; and so on. *117 rue Dalhousie.* ☎ *418/692-4555. www. laurieraphael. com. Entrees C$38–C$54. AE, DC, DISC, MC, V. Lunch & dinner Tues–Fri, dinner Sat.*

★ kids **Le Café du Monde** *TRADI-TIONAL FRENCH* Large (it seats more than 200) and jovial, this very Parisian-style restaurant manages the nearly impossible: classic French food and fast service without a compromise in quality—even on crowded holiday weekends. *84 rue Dalhousie.* ☎ *418/692-4455. www.lecafedu monde.com. Entrees C$14–C$30. AE, DC, MC, V. Lunch & dinner daily, breakfast Sat–Sun and holidays.*

★★ **Le Clocher Penché Bistrot** *BISTRO* The development of this unpretentious St-Roch neighborhood bistro parallels the polishing up of the overall area. With its caramel-toned woods, tall ceilings, and walls serving as gallery space for local artists, Clocher Penché has laid-back European class. Service reflects the food—amiable and without flourishes. *203 rue St-Joseph est.* ☎ *418/640-0597. Entrees C$19–C$26. MC, V. Lunch & dinner Tues–Sat, brunch Sun.*

★★ **L'Echaudé** *BISTRO* In a city that specializes in the informal bistro tradition, L'Echaudé is a star. The classic dishes are all in place, from confit de canard to steak frites, and the tone is casual sophistication. *73 rue Sault-au-Matelot.* ☎ *418/692-1299. Entrees C$25–C$35. AE, DC, MC, V. Lunch & dinner daily.*

The bustling Le Café du Monde.

Elegant but not overbearing, L'Echaudé stands out, even in Québec's bistro-packed dining scene.

★★ **kids** **Le Pain Béni** CONTEMPORARY QUEBECOIS Québécois classics with modern twists, such as sweetbreads and red tuna caramelized in honey and soy with a vanilla-perfumed artichoke purée. Desserts are especially creative, such as lemon pie splash featuring a lemony homemade marshmallow. *24 rue Ste-Anne.* ☎ *418/694-9485. www.auberge placedarmes.com. Entrees C$14–C$45. AE, DC, MC, V. Lunch & dinner daily.*

★ **Mistral Gagnant** BISTRO This "restaurant Provençal" channels the spirit of a modest village cafe in France, in both its sunny decor and its friendly atmosphere. Better yet, the food is fairly priced and tasty. The menu, which might include flakey white sea bass with pesto and carrot mousse, changes daily. *160 rue St. Paul.* ☎ *418/692-4260. www. mistralgagnant.ca. Entrees C$15–C$31. AE, MC, V. Lunch & dinner Tues–Sat.*

★★ **Panache** CONTEMPORARY QUEBECOIS The restaurant of the superb Auberge Saint-Antoine (p 140) is housed in a former 19th-century warehouse delineated by massive wood beams and rough stone walls. It is the most romantic of the city. The frequently changing menu is

heavy on locally sourced game, duck, and fish. *10 rue St-Antoine.* ☎ *418/692-1022. www.saint-antoine.com. Entrees C$43–C$50. AE, DC, MC, V. Breakfast & dinner daily, lunch Wed–Fri.*

★ **kids** **Ristorante Il Teatro** ITALIAN Boasting a huge menu (22 types of pasta and six types of risotto, for example), generous portions, and fair prices, this convivial restaurant also has a large sidewalk cafe and a *table du soir*, making it one of the few places to get a meal until 11pm or even later. *972 rue St-Jean.* ☎ *418/694-9996. www.le capitole.com/en/restaurant.php. Entrees C$12–C$36. AE, DC, MC, V. Breakfast, lunch & dinner daily.*

★ **Toast!** CONTEMPORARY QUEBECOIS The outdoor dining terrace in back, with wrought-iron furniture and big leafy trees overhead, is an oasis. The interior room glows crimson from a wall of fire-engine-red tiles, retro-modern lights, and red Plexiglas window paneling. *17 rue Sault-au-Matelot.* ☎ *418/692-1334. www.restauranttoast.com. Table d'hôte only C$65, C$75, or C$85. AE, DC, MC, V. Dinner daily.*

Tourists take in a trompe l'oeil mural depicting citizens of the early city.

The Laurentians

1 St-Sauveur

2 Val David

3 Mont-Tremblant
  Pedestrian Village

4 A Day at
  Le Scandinave Spa

Where to Stay

Château Beauvallon 10

Fairmont Mont-Tremblant 5

Hôtel Mont-Tremblant 8

Quintessence 9

Where to Dine

Aux Truffes 6

Crêperie Catherine 7

T he Laurentian Mountains (also known as the Laurentides) provide year-round recreational opportunities. Skiing and snowboarding are the most popular activities, but in the warmer months the mountains thaw and open up a new array of options. The highest peak, Mont-Tremblant, is 968m (3,176 ft.) high and located 129km (80 miles) northwest of Montréal. Closer to the city, the terrain resembles a rumpled quilt, its folds and hollows cupping a multitude of lakes. Come for a day or stay for a week. Note that as you head north, you're more likely to find venues whose proprietors and websites are French only. **START: Drive north out of Montréal on Autoroute 15. For an orientation to the region, stop at the information center, well marked from the highway, at exit 51. Tourisme Laurentides (☎ 800/561-6673; www.laurentides.com) shares a building with a 24-hour McDonald's.**

① **St-Sauveur.** Only 60km (37 miles) north of Montréal, the village of St-Sauveur is flush with outlet malls and the carloads of shoppers they attract, while a few blocks farther north, the older village square bustles with less-frenzied activity. Dining and snacking on everything from crepes to hot dogs are big activities here, evidenced by the many beckoning cafes. If you want a picnic, Chez Bernard (411 rue Principale; ☎ 450/240-0000; www.chez bernard.com) is a pretty store that sells fragrant cheeses, crusty breads, savory tarts, pâtés, sausages, and prepared meals. You'll want to fill up before heading to Parc Aquatique du Mont St-Sauveur (☎ 450/227-4671; www.parcaquatique.com), Canada's largest water park. It features rafting, a wave pool, a tidal-wave river, and slides, including one which you travel to by chairlift and ride down in a tube. Full-day tickets are C$14 to C$35, with half-day and family rates also available. For 10 days in August, the Festival des Art de St-Sauveur (☎ 450/227-0427; www.fass.ca) presents music and dance performances along with jazz and chamber concerts. The schedule always includes a number of free events.

② **Val David.** This is the region's faintly bohemian enclave, conjuring up images of cabin hideaways set among ponds and lakes, while creeks tumble through fragrant forests. There are hectares of breathtaking trails for mountain bikers and hikers (and, in winter, snowshoers and cross-country skiers), and Val David is one of the villages along the bike path called P'Tit Train du Nord, built on a former railroad track (see "Biker's Paradise: The Route Verte," below). Residents boast that Val David is the birthplace of rock climbing in Eastern Canada, and climbing enthusiasts flock to the nearby Dufresne Regional Park (www. parcregionaldufresne.com) to

A home in sleepy Val David, a mecca for skiers in winter and hikers in summer.

You'll find charming villages and fantastic ski slopes in the Mont-Tremblant area.

explore its 650 rated routes. Unlike the heavily visited Mont-Tremblant, where cheesy souvenir stores are plentiful, Val David is home to a handful of stylish little stores that sell well-made, authentic crafts. If you're in the area from mid-July to mid-August, check out the village's huge ceramic art festival (☎ 819/322-6868; www.1001pots.com). Sculptors and ceramicists, along with painters, jewelers, pewter smiths, and other craftspeople display their work; and there are concerts and other outdoor activities including pottery workshops for children on weekends. *Tourist office at 2579 rue de l'Église.* ☎ 888/322-7030. www.valdavid.com.

❸ **Mont-Tremblant Pedestrian Village.** The Mont-Tremblant area is a kind of Aspen meets Disneyland. A terrific ski mountain boasts an ever-expanding resort village at the bottom of its slope and is a prime destination in the province in all four seasons. The Mont-Tremblant ski resort (www.tremblant.ca) draws the biggest downhill crowds in the Laurentians and is repeatedly ranked as the top resort in eastern North America by *Ski Magazine* (see "Skiing in the Laurentians," below). There are some well-regarded cultural offerings here, too, including the Tremblant International Blues

Festival (www.tremblantblues.com), which puts on up to 150 free shows for 10 days in July. The village itself has the prefabricated look of a theme park, but at least planners used the Québécois architectural style of pitched roofs in bright colors, not ersatz Bavarian Alpine flourishes. For a sweeping view, take the free gondola from the bottom of the village to the top. It zips over the walkways, candy-colored hotels, and outdoor swimming pools. There are dozens of restaurants, bars, and shops here, and most are open year-round. *Tourisme de Mont-Tremblant, 5080 Montée Ryan.* ☎ 819/425-2434. www.tourismemont tremblant.com.

❹ **A Day at the Spa.** Spas are big business around here. They're the most popular new features at hotels, especially in the Mont-Tremblant area, where people are looking for new ways to pamper themselves beyond dropping a lot of money on skiing. In the Québec province, the organization Spas Relais Santé distinguishes between day spas, which offer massages and *esthétique* services such as facials; destination spas, which often involve overnight stays and healthy cuisine; and Nordic spas, which are built around a natural water source

A summer sail on Lac Tremblant is a peaceful and scenic way to spend an afternoon.

Biker's Paradise: The Route Verte

In 2007, Québec province officially inaugurated the Route Verte (Green Route), a 4,000km (2,485-mile) bike network that stretches from one end of the province to the other, linking all regions and cities. The idea was modeled on the Rails-to-Trails program in the U.S. and cycling routes in Denmark, Great Britain, and along the Danube and Rhine rivers. Within a year, the National Geographic Society had declared it one of the 10 best bicycle routes in the world.

Included in the network is the popular P'tit Train du Nord bike trail through the Laurentian Mountains. It's built on a former railway track and passes through the villages of Ste-Adèle, Val David, and Mont-Tremblant. Cyclists can get food and bike repairs at renovated railway stations along the way and hop on for a day trip or a longer tour. The trail is free to ride on. The Route Verte website (www.routeverte.com) provides maps and an "accommodations" link that lists places to rent bikes as well as B&Bs, campsites, and hotels that are especially focused on serving travelers. The annual official tourist guide to the Laurentians published by the regional tourist office (☎ 800/561-6673 or 450/224-7007; www.laurentides.com) always has a big section on biking. If you plan a trip, keep in mind Transport du Parc Linéaire (☎ 888/686-1323 or 450/569-5596; www.transportduparclineaire.com), which provides baggage transport from inn to inn.

and include outdoor and indoor spaces.

If you've never experienced a European-style Nordic spa before, try to set aside 3 hours for a visit to Le Scandinave Spa (4280 Montée Ryan, Mont-Tremblant; ☎ 888/537-2263 or 891/425-5524; www.scandinave.com). It's a tranquil complex of small buildings tucked among evergreen trees on the Diable River shore, and is as chic as it is rustic. For C$43 Monday to Friday or C$45 Saturday to Sunday, visitors (18 and older only) have the run of the facility. Options include outdoor hot tubs designed to look like natural pools (one is set under a manmade waterfall); a Norwegian steam bath thick with eucalyptus scent; indoor relaxation areas with super-comfortable, low-slung chairs; and

the river itself, which the heartiest of folk dip into even on frigid winter days. (A heat lamp keeps a small square of river open on the iciest of days.) The idea is to move from hot to cold to hot, which supposedly purges toxins and invigorates your skin. Bathing suits are required, and men and women share all spaces except the changing rooms. For extra fees, massages and yoga classes are offered.

Couples, mothers and daughters, groups of friends, and folks on their own all come to "take the waters." The spa is year-round, and few activities are more delicious than being in a warm outdoor pool as snow falls, the sun sets, and the temperature plummets. (That stroll back to the locker room, however, is another story.)

The Laurentians: **Where to Stay in Mont-Tremblant**

The lodge-style lobby of the Fairmont Mont-Tremblant, one of the best resorts in the Laurentians.

★★ **kids** **Château Beauvallon** Since opening in 2005, Beauvallon has become the region's premiere property for families who want to stay near but off the ski mountain. The 70-suite operation positions itself as an affordable high-end retreat for seasoned travelers, and delivers with a relaxed elegance. *6385 Montée Ryan.* ☎ *888/681-6611 or 819/681-6611. www.chateau beauvallon.com. 70 units. Doubles C$179–C$239. AE, DC, MC, V.*

★★ **kids** **Fairmont Mont-Tremblant** The name-brand resort for families who want to stay directly on the mountain. The Fairmont stands on a crest above the pedestrian village and offers year-round outdoor and indoor pools, a 38-person outdoor Jacuzzi, and ski-in, ski-out accessibility to the chairlifts. *3045 chemin de la Chapelle.* ☎ *800/257-7544 or 819/681-7000. www. fairmont.com/tremblant. 314 units. Doubles C$249–C$369. AE, DC, DISC, MC, V.*

Hôtel Mont-Tremblant Located in the old village of Mont-Tremblant 5km (3 miles) northwest of the pedestrian village, this modest hotel is popular with skiers who want to avoid the resort village's higher prices and cyclists who appreciate the location directly on the Route Verte bike path. Rates include dinner. *1900 chemin du Village (Rte. 327).* ☎ *888/887-1111 or 819/425-3232. www.hotelmonttremblant.com. 22 units. Doubles C$169 w/dinner. AE, MC, V.*

★★★ **Quintessence** The region's luxury property. Every room is a suite, accommodations are hugely comfortable, there's an outdoor infinity pool, and the spa is reserved for hotel guests only. Lavish dinners can be taken in the intimate Jardin des Saveurs or La Quintessence dining room, or outdoors near the pool. *3004 chemin de la Chapelle.* ☎ *866/425-3400 or 819/425-3400. www. hotelquintessence.com. 30 units. Suites C$450–C$1,630. AE, MC, V.*

The Laurentians: **Where to Dine in Mont-Tremblant**

★★ **Aux Truffes** *FRENCH CONTEMPORARY* Aux Truffes offers perfectly executed French cuisine.

One of the many delicious dishes at Aux Truffes.

Imaginative mains include a roasted rack of caribou served "shepherd's-pie" style with *chicoutai* berries sauce. *Place Saint-Bernard, 3035 chemin de la Chapelle (in the pedestrian village).* ☎ *819/681-4544. www.auxtruffes.com. Entrees C$29–C$46. AE, MC, V. Dinner daily.*

Crêperie Catherine BREAKFAST/ BRUNCH In addition to both savory and sweet crepes made before your eyes, Crêperie Catherine has cultivated something neighboring restaurants lack—cozy ambience. Don't hesitate to smother your crepe with the house specialty, *sucre a la crème* (a concoction of brown sugar and butter). *113 chemin Kandahar (in the pedestrian village).* ☎ *819/681-4888.*

Part of the charm of visiting the Laurentians is driving through the region's picturesque towns.

www.creperiecatherine.ca. Entrees C$12–C$17, dessert crepes from C$4.95. Breakfast, lunch & dinner daily.

Skiing in the Laurentians

Founded in 1939 by a Philadelphia millionaire named Joe Ryan, the Mont-Tremblant ski resort pioneered the development of trails on both sides of a mountain and was the second mountain in the world to install a chairlift. Today, the vertical drop is 645m (2,116 ft.), and there are 94 downhill runs and trails. Half are expert terrain, about a third are intermediate, and the rest beginner. The longest trail, Nansen, is 6km (almost 4 miles). The resort has snowmaking capability to cover almost three-quarters of its skiable terrain—255 hectares (630 acres).

When the snow is deep, skiers here like to follow the sun around the mountain, making the run down slopes with an eastern exposure in the morning and down the western-facing ones in the afternoon. There are higher mountains elsewhere with longer runs and steeper pitches, but something about Mont-Tremblant compels people to return time and again.

Cross-country skiers have many options. Parc National du Mont-Tremblant boasts 10 loops (53km/33 miles) of groomed track in the Diable sector, and as of winter 2009 the Pimbina sector is designated exclusively for snowshoeing and backcountry skiing. Visit www.sepaq.com to locate visitor centers and information kiosks or to check availability of the five new yurts, which sleep four in any season.

Skiers, snowboarders, and other winter sports enthusiasts flock to the Laurentians' world-class slopes.

Cantons-de-l'Est

Knowlton 1
Magog 2
The Bleu Lavende Farm 3

Where to Stay
Manoir des Sables 4
Manoir Hovey 6

Where to Dine
Boulangerie Owl's Bread 5
Pilsen Restaurant & Pub 7

QUÉBEC

CANTONS-DE-L'EST

CENTRE-DU-QUÉBEC

MONTÉRÉGIE

MONTRÉAL

NEW HAMPSHIRE

MAINE

VERMONT

NEW YORK

UNITED STATES

CANADA

Parc du Mt-Orford

Parc de la Yamaska

Grand L. Brompton

Mont-Orford

L. Brome

Lake Memphrémagog

Lake Champlain

St. Lawrence

L. Massawippi

L. Magog

Victoriaville

Weedon-Centre

Scotstown

Sherbrooke

Windsor

Richmond

Drummondville

Saint-Hyacinthe

Granby

Bromont

Waterloo

Magog

North Hatley

Hatley

Coaticook

Ayer's Cliff

Stanstead Canton

Knowlton

Lac-Brome

St-Benoît-Du-Lac

Sutton

Dunham

West Brome

Cowansville

Chambly

Saint-Luc

Boucherville

Longueuil

St-Jean-sur-Richelieu

Napierville

Châteauguay

161

212

3

112

161

55

116

20

55

10

112

104

202

133

133

30

40

25

20

10

15

40

158

15

138

91

141

55

The rolling countryside of Cantons-de-l'Est is largely pastoral, marked by rolling hills, small villages, a smattering of vineyards, and the 792m (2,598-ft.) peak of Mont-Orford, the centerpiece of a provincial park. Serene glacial lakes attract summer swimmers, boaters, and bicyclists who loop around them. In winter, skiers who don't head north to the Laurentians come this direction. Still referred to by most Anglophones as the Eastern Townships, the southern edge of the region borders Vermont, New Hampshire, and Maine.

START: **Leave Montréal by Pont Champlain, the bridge which funnels into arrow-straight Autoroute 10, and head east toward Sherbrooke.**

❶ **Knowlton.** For a good confluence of countryside, cafes, and antiquing, head to the town of Knowlton, at Brome Lake's southeast corner. It's part of the seven-village municipality known as Lac Brome. From Autoroute 10, take exit 90, heading south on Rte. 243. Two main shopping streets (Lakeside and Knowlton) have about three dozen boutiques and antiques stores that reveal the creeping chic influence of refugees from Montréal. For a quick snack, the funky, barnlike Station Knowlton Country Store (7 Mount Echo Rd.; ☎ 450/242-5862; www.stationknowlton.com) sells fruit smoothies and healthy sandwiches.

❷ **Magog.** Confusingly, the town of Magog is not adjacent to Lac Magog. That lake is about 13km (8 miles) north. Instead, the town is positioned at the northernmost end of the long Lac Memphrémagog, which spills across the U.S.-Canadian border into Vermont on its southern end. Croisière Memphrémagog (☎ 888/842-8068 or 819/843-8068; www.croisiere-memphremagog. com) offers lake cruises leaving from Point Merry Park, the focal point for many of the town's outdoor activities. Several firms rent sailboats, motorboats, kayaks, and windsurfers. The town is one of the largest in the region, with about 25,000 people and lots of boutiques and chic

The monks at the Abbaye de Saint-Benoît-du-Lac make and sell a variety of popular cheeses.

Cabanes à Sucre: A Little Old Place Where We Can Get Together

Throughout Canada's history, maple syrup has been an economic and cultural boon for the Québec province. In March and April, maple trees around Montréal are tapped and *cabanes à sucre* (sugar shacks) open up in rural areas. Some just sell maple syrup and candies, while many serve full meals and even stage entertainment.

A particularly fun tradition is *tire sur la neige,* where hot maple syrup is poured onto a clean layer of snow. Guests pick up the semisoft confection before it hardens and enjoy what's known as "maple toffee."

The region's delicious maple syrup is a widely used ingredient in area restaurants.

restaurants. Not far from here is Abbaye de Saint-Benoît-du-Lac (☎ 819/843-4080; www.st-benoit-du-lac.com), a monastery that's home to about 50 monks who live largely in silence. They support themselves by making cheeses and products from their apple orchards, which are sold on-site in a small shop. Visitors also can attend services that feature Gregorian chant.

❸ The Bleu Lavende Farm. Canada's largest producer of lavender also happens to be one of the region's most popular destinations.

Bleu Lavende (☎ 888/876-5851 or 819/876-5851; www.bleulavande.ca) is a huge farm, an agricultural discovery center, and a place to buy products infused with lavandula: chocolate, cleaning products, sprays, and other goodies. Located on 891 Narrow Rd., 4.4km (2.7 miles) from Rte. 247 in Stanstead, it can attract more than 2,000 visitors per day during peak season, when the lavender blooms in July and August. The boutique is open daily during high season and Monday to Friday during low season.

Cantons-de-l'Est: **Where to Stay**

★★ Manoir des Sables ORFORD This facility is one of the region's most complete resort hotels, and its unofficial motto could be "we have something for everyone." It serves couples, families, golfers, skiers, skaters, fitness players, and kayakers, and offers up snowshoeing, on-site ice skating, and Saturday-night horse-drawn sleigh rides in winter, with canoeing and fishing in the hotel's lake in summer. *90 av. des Jardins.* ☎ *800/567-3514 or 819/847-4747. www.manoir dessables.com. 141 units. Doubles C$178–C$250. AE, DC, MC, V.*

The rooms at the Manoir Hovey are elegant and refined.

★★★ Manoir Hovey NORTH

HATLEY This manor, a member of the exclusive Relais & Châteaux group, manages to maintain a magical balance of feeling between a genteel estate for a private getaway and a grand resort for a weekend's pampering. Aristocratic touches include tea and scones in the afternoon, a carefully manicured English garden, and a massive stone hearth in a library lounge. Its restaurant is the most esteemed in the region. *575 chemin Hovey.* ☎ *800/661-2421 or 819/842-2421. www.manoirhovey. com. 41 units. Doubles C$320–C$590 w/breakfast, 3-course dinner, gratuities, and use of most recreational facilities. AE, DC, MC, V.*

Cantons-de-l'Est: **Where to Dine**

★ Boulangerie Owl's Bread

MAGOG *FRENCH* This bakery and restaurant serves up mouth-watering pastries for breakfast and a sit-down lunch every day. Try the cassoulet Toulousain or the "Eastern Township style" panini which features smoked Lake Brome duck breast, blue cheese from nearby Abbaye de Saint-Benoît-du-Lac, Grenoble walnuts, and a touch of maple syrup. *428 rue Principale ouest.* ☎ *819/847-1987. www.*

owlsbread.com. Most items under C$13. MC, V. Breakfast & lunch daily.

Pilsen Restaurant & Pub

NORTH HATLEY *INTERNATIONAL* Featuring a deck over a narrow river, this former horse-carriage manufacturing shop fills up quickly on warm days with patrons dining on quesadillas, burgers, pastas, fried calamari, and the Ploughman's Platter with wild game terrine, Abbaye de Saint-Benoît-du-Lac blue

Wine (*& Cidre de Glace*) Country

Canada is known more for its beers than its wines, but that hasn't stopped agriculturists from giving wine a shot. In Cantons-de-l'Est, vintners are concentrated around Dunham, about 103km (64 miles) southeast of Montréal, with several vineyards along Rte. 202. A stop for a snack or a facility tour makes for a pleasant afternoon, and if you're really gung-ho, follow the established Route des Vins (www.laroutedesvins.ca), which passes 16 vintners. One farm on the route is Vignoble de l'Orpailleur (1086 Rte. 202, Dunham; ☎ 450/295-2763; www.orpailleur.ca), which has guided tours daily from June through October. Its L'Orpailleur Classique is popular on Montréal restaurant menus.

Ice cider and ice wine are two regional products that may be new to visitors. They're made from apples and grapes left on trees and vines past the first frost, and are served ice-cold with cheese, foie gras, or dessert. A top producer is Domaine Pinnacle (150 Richford Rd., Frelighsburg; ☎ 450/298-1226; www.icecider.com), about 13km (8 miles) south of Dunham. Its *cidre de glace* is a regular gold medalist in international competitions. The farm's tasting room and boutique are open daily from 10am to 6pm May through December.

cheese pâté, onion confit, and apples (washed down by local microbrew Massawippi Blonde, natch). **55 rue Main.** ☎ 819/842-2971. *www.pilsen.ca. Entrees C$10–C$27. AE, MC, V. Lunch & dinner daily mid-May to Nov, Thurs–Sun rest of the year.* ●

The region's maple trees are tapped by syrup producers every March and April.

The **Savvy Traveler**

Before You Go

Government Tourist Offices

In Montréal: Downtown Montréal boasts a large **Infotouriste Centre** (1255 rue Peel; toll free from the U.S. ☎ **877/266-5687;** toll from the U.K. ☎ **0800/051-7055** or 514/873-2015). The city of Montréal maintains a terrific website at **www.tourisme-montreal.org**.

In the U.S.: The main Québec tourist information office is the **Québec Government Office in New York** (One Rockefeller Plaza, 26th Floor, New York, NY 10020; ☎ **212/843-0950**). Branch offices are listed at the agency's website, **www.quebec usa.org**.

In the U.K.: Contact the **Québec Government Office in London** (59 Pall Mall, London SW1Y 5JH; ☎ **44-207/766-5900; www.quebec.org.uk**).

The Best Times to Go

The summer months—late June through August—are when Montréal is at its busiest. You'll pay the most for a hotel room in this period, and it can be hot and humid, but the city is in full bloom. In May and early June it's easier to get accommodations and the weather is often more comfortable, although you'll miss out on the big festivals. September and October are less hectic months and the perfect time for autumn hikes and seeing the region's beautiful fall foliage. Winter in Montréal is cold and snowy, but people still get out and play. The worst times to visit are early spring and late fall, when the weather can get iffy and not much is happening.

Festivals & Special Events

JANUARY. **La Fête des Neiges** (Snow Festival; ☎ **514/872-6120;** www.fetedesneiges.com) is the city's premier winter festival and features outdoor events such as harness racing, barrel jumping, ice sculpting, snowshoeing, skating, and cross-country skiing.

FEBRUARY. **The Festival Montréal en Lumière,** or Montréal High Lights Festival (☎ **888/477-9955** or 514/288-9955; www.montreal highlights.com) is a deep-winter food fest with culinary competitions and wine tastings, multimedia light shows, classical and pop concerts, and a Montréal All-Nighter that ends with a free breakfast at dawn.

MAY. **Montréal Museums Day** (www.museesmontreal.org), on the last Sunday in May, is a day of free admission to most of the city's museums. There even are free buses to get visitors from place to place.

JUNE. **Montréal Bike Fest** (☎ **800/567-8356** or 514/521-8356; www.velo.qc.ca) brings out tens of thousands of cyclists for races of varying degrees of length and difficulty over 8 days, attracting over 100,000 spectators. Also in June, the **Saint-Ambroise Montréal Fringe Festival** (☎ **514/849-3378;** www.montrealfringe.ca) is 10 days of out-there theater with acts such as a one-man Star Wars stand-up, clowns gone bad, and drunken drag queens (for a long time, the event's website featured a hand raising its middle finger).

JULY. Hordes of sightseers and music fans make the **Festival International de Jazz de Montréal** (☎ **888/515-0515** or 514/871-1881; www.montrealjazzfest.com) one of the most exciting in the world. At the **Festival Juste pour Rire,** or Just for Laughs festival (☎ **888/244-3155** or

MONTRÉAL'S AVERAGE MONTHLY TEMPERATURES (°F/°C)

	JAN	FEB	MAR	APR	MAY	JUNE
High (°F)	21	24	35	51	65	73
(°C)	−6	−4	2	11	18	23
	79	76	66	54	41	27
	26	24	19	12	5	−3
	JULY	AUG	SEPT	OCT	NOV	DEC
Low (°F)	7	10	21	35	47	56
(°C)	−14	−12	−6	2	8	13
	61	59	50	39	29	13
	16	15	10	4	−2	−11

514/845-2322; www.hahaha.com), improvisational comedy by known and lesser-known names keeps the city in stitches. For about a dozen evenings over the summer, the **International Fireworks Competition** (☎ 514/397-2000; www. internationaldesfeuxloto-quebec. com) lights up the skies with 30-minute shows. Also in July, the gay and lesbian community's huge annual pride celebration, **Diver/Cité** (☎ 514/285-4011; www.diverscite. org) presents 8 days of dance, drag, art, and music concerts, with nearly everything outdoors and free.

AUGUST. The **Festival des Films du Monde** (☎ 514/848-3883; www. ffm-montreal.org) has been an international film event since 1977. A strong panel of actors, directors, and writers from around the world make up the jury each year, giving the event a weight that many festivals lack.

SEPTEMBER. It's the perfect time of year to view the fall foliage in the city's parks and the surrounding region, especially the northern Laurentian Mountains (p 144).

OCTOBER. One of the biggest gay events on the planet, the **Black & Blue Festival** (☎ 514/875-7026; www.bbcm.org), was, a few years ago, named the best international

fest by France's Pink TV Awards, beating out even Carnival in Rio. And when we say big, we mean big: The main event is an all-night party at Olympic Stadium. There's also a Jock Ball, a Leather Ball, and a Military Ball.

DECEMBER. Celebrating the holidays a la française is a particular treat in Vieux-Montréal, where the streets are nearly always banked with snow and ancient buildings sport wreaths, decorated fir trees, and glittery white lights.

The Weather

It's a city of extremes when it comes to the weather. There are two main seasons in Montréal: a hot summer and a bitterly cold winter. About 3 weeks of pleasant spring and crisp fall take place in between. For the current weather forecast, call ☎ **514/283-3010** or check www. weatheroffice.gc.ca.

Useful Websites

- **www.tourisme-montreal.org**: The slick official site of the city, with up-to-the-minute details and information about venues, festivals, neighborhoods, and hotel deals. It has special sections for gay and lesbian travelers, who make up a big part of the tourism business.

- **http://montrealplus.ca**: Yellow Pages–style listings that include small yet useful descriptions of clubs, restaurants, shops, and more.

- **www.cbc.ca/montreal**: The Canadian Broadcasting Corporation's minisite of news of the city.

- **www.montrealgazette.com**: The city's English-language newspaper. A bit heavy on tabloid-style reporting, but a useful source of restaurant and cultural happenings.

- **www.montrealmirror.com**: Montréal's best weekly alternative publication, featuring concert listings and entertainment articles.

- **www.stm.info**: Montréal's public transportation system. Check here for detailed route maps of bus and Métro lines and information on service interruptions. A useful trip planner helps you figure out the best combinations of public transport to get from one place to another.

Cellphones

Visitors from the U.S. should be able to get roaming service that allows them to use their cellphones in Canada. Some wireless companies allow customers to adjust their plans for cheaper rates while traveling. Sprint, for instance, has a "Canadian roaming" option for US$3 per month that reduces the per-minute rate to US20¢. Europeans and other travelers on the GSM (Global System for Mobile Communications) network may be able to purchase pay-as-you-go SIM cards in Canada. Call your wireless provider for information.

Cellphone rentals are not common in Canada, so if you end up traveling without a phone, online phone services are your best option. With OneSuite.com (☎ 866/417-8483; www.onesuite.com), for instance, you prepay an online account and then dial a toll-free or local access number when traveling, enter your PIN, then dial the number you're calling. Calls from Canada to mainland U.S. cost US2.5¢ to US3.5¢ per minute. Calls to the U.K. cost 2p per minute to a landline and 17.5p per minute to a mobile.

Car Rentals

If you're arriving in town by train or plane, you won't need a car in Montréal unless you plan on taking day trips outside the city limits. Even then you should wait to rent until you're actually ready to head out. Free parking can be scarce on city streets.

All the major car-rental companies are represented in Montréal. You'll find rental agencies downtown as well as at Montréal-Trudeau airport. The best deals are usually found online at rental-car company websites, although all the major online travel agencies also offer rental-car reservations services. Websites for car-rental agencies are listed later in this chapter.

Québec is the first Canadian province to mandate that residents have radial snow tires on their cars in winter. The law, which debuted in late 2008, runs from mid-December until March 15. Rental-car agencies are required to provide snow tires on car rentals during that period, and many charge an extra, non-negotiable fee.

Getting **There**

By Plane

Montréal's main airport is **Aéroport International Pierre-Elliot-Trudeau de Montréal** (airport code YUL; ☎ 800/465-1213 or 514/394-7377; www.admtl.com), known better as Montréal-Trudeau airport. It's 23km (14 miles) southwest of downtown Montréal.

It's served by the shuttle bus L'Aérobus (☎ 514/631-1856), which travels between the airport and downtown, stopping at Berri Terminal, the city's main bus terminal, also known as the Station Centrale d'Autobus. Buses run daily every 30 minutes from 9am to 8:30pm and every hour from 9pm to 9am. One-way fares are C$15 for adults. The ride takes about 30 minutes.

A taxi trip to downtown Montréal costs a flat fare of C$38 plus tip. Call ☎ 514/394-7377 for more information.

By Car

Many visitors from the mid-Atlantic and New England regions of the United States and eastern sections of Canada drive to Montréal. All international drivers must carry a valid driver's license from their country of residence. A U.S. license is sufficient as long as you are a visitor and actually are a U.S. resident. A U.K. license is sufficient as well. If the driver's license is in a language other than French or English, an International Driver's Permit is required in conjunction with the country of residence driver's license.

Driving north to Montréal from the U.S., the entire journey is on expressways. From New York City, all but the last 40 or so miles of the 603km (375-mile) journey are within New York State on I-87. I-87 links up with Canada's Autoroute 15 at the border, which goes straight to Montréal. From Boston, I-93 goes up through New Hampshire's White Mountains and merges into I-91 to cross the tip of Vermont. At the border, I-91 becomes Autoroute 55. Signs lead to Autoroute 10 west, which goes into Montréal. From Boston to Montréal is 518km (322 miles).

By Train

Montréal is a major terminus on Canada's **VIA Rail** network (☎ 888/842-7245 or 514/989-2626; www.viarail.ca). Its station, **Gare Centrale** (895 rue de la Gauchetière ouest; ☎ 514/989-2626), is centrally located downtown. The station is connected to the Métro subway system at **Bonaventure Station.** VIA Rail trains are comfortable—all major routes have Wi-Fi, and some trains are equipped with dining cars and sleeping cars.

Amtrak (☎ 800/872-7245; www.amtrak.com) has one train per day into Montréal from New York that makes intermediate stops. Called the Adirondack, it's very slow, but its scenic route passes along the Hudson River's eastern shore and west of Lake Champlain. The Adirondack takes 11 hours from New York if all goes well, but delays aren't unusual.

By Bus

Montréal's central bus station is **Station Centrale d'Autobus** (505 bd. de Maisonneuve est; ☎ 514/842-2281). Beneath the terminal is **Berri-UQAM Station,** the junction of several Métro lines. Greyhound (☎ 800/231-2222; www.greyhound.com) is among the operators with routes from Boston and New York to Montréal. The trip from Boston takes as little as 7 hours; from New York City, 8 hours. The seats are more cramped and the views a little less scenic than what you'll get on a train, but the bus makes fewer stops en route and you'll often get through the border crossing faster, making the trip significantly shorter than the train ride.

Getting **Around**

On Foot

Montréal is a terrific walking city. One thing to keep in mind when strolling is to be sure to cross only at street corners and only when you have a green light or a walk sign. City police began cracking down on jay-walkers in 2007 in an attempt to cut down on the number of accidents involving pedestrians, and newspapers continue to carry stories of fines being issued. Be careful in the wintertime, too, when sidewalks and roadways can be extremely icy.

By Public Transportation

For speed and economy, nothing beats Montréal's **Métro system** (STM; ☎ **514/786-4636;** www.stm. info). Modeled after the system in Paris, it consists of four color-coded main lines, and is clean, reliable, and simple to use. Stations are marked on the street by blue-and-white signs that show a circle enclosing a down-pointing arrow. The Métro runs from about 5:30am to 1am.

Fares are by the ride, not by distance. Single rides cost C$2.75. A card with six rides costs C$12.75, and a weekly pass, good for unlimited rides, is C$20. Reduced fares are available for children and, with special Métro OPUS cards, for seniors and students. Sales are cash only. You can buy tickets from the booth attendant in any station or from a convenience store.

Tourist Cards can be a good deal if you plan to use the Métro more than three times in 1 day. You get unlimited access to the bus and Métro network for 1 day for C$9 or 3 consecutive days for C$17. The front of the card has scratch-off sections like a lottery ticket—you scratch out the month and day (or 3 consecutive days) which you wish to use the card on.

To enter the system, slip your ticket into the slot in the turnstile, show your pass to the booth attendant, or hand your ticket to the attendant. If you plan to transfer to a bus, take a transfer ticket (correspondence) from the machine just inside the turnstile; every Métro station has one, and it allows you a free transfer to a bus wherever you exit the subway.

City buses, also run by STM, aren't quite as efficient as the Métro, though they do run to places that the Métro doesn't stop. Some routes also run late at night (if on a limited schedule), after the Métro has shut down for the evening. The STM website has a trip-planning feature to help you plot out which combination of subways and buses to take to your destination. The cost of a bus ride is the same as for the Métro, and you can use the same cards and tickets. If you want to pay in cash, you need to have exact change.

By Taxi

There's no single general taxi company in the city, and taxis come in all shapes, sizes, and colors. As a result, the only way to distinguish a taxi from a normal car is the illuminated sign on its roof. Taxis line up outside most large hotels or can be hailed on the street. Members of hotel and restaurant staffs can also

Tap Your Own Pedal Power

Montréal is bike crazy, and it's got the goods to justify it. The city helps people indulge their passions by overseeing an ever-expanding network of **560km (348 miles) of cycling paths** and year-round bike lanes. From April to November, car lanes in heavily biked areas are blocked off with concrete barriers, turning the passages into two-way lanes for bikers. Most Métro stations have large bike racks, and in some neighborhoods sections of the street where cars would normally park are fenced off for bike parking.

If you're serious about cycling, get in touch with the nonprofit biking organization **Vélo Québec** (☎ 800/567-8356 or 514/521-8356; www.velo.qc.ca). Its main office, **La Maison des Cyclists** (1251 rue Rachel), is located directly on Parc La Fontaine. It has a cafe with indoor and outdoor tables, a boutique with books and bike gear, and staff to help arrange bike trips and tours. The bicycle rental shop **Cycle Pop** (1000 rue Rachel est; ☎ 514/526-2525; www.cyclepop.ca) is just down the block. Other rental shops around the city include **ÇaRoule/Montréal on Wheels** (p 52) in Vieux-Montréal.

call cabs, many of which are dispatched by radio.

The initial charge is C\$3.30. Each additional kilometer (⅔ mile) adds C\$1.60, and each minute of waiting adds C\$.60. A short ride from one point to another downtown usually costs about C\$7. Tip about 10% to 15%.

Montréal taxi drivers range in temperament from unstoppably loquacious to sullen and cranky. Some know their city well, others have sketchy knowledge and poor language skills, so it's a good idea to have your destination written down—with the cross street—to show your driver.

By Car
Montréal is an easy city to navigate by car, although traffic during morning and late afternoon rush hour can be horrendous. Avoid the busy rue Ste-Catherine and opt for boulevard René Lévesque if you want to travel east-west through downtown. All familiar rules apply, though turning right on red in the city is prohibited.

It can be difficult to park for free in downtown Montréal, but there are plenty of metered spaces. Traditional meters are set well back from the curb so they won't be buried by plowed snow in winter. Metered parking costs C\$3 per hour, and meters are in effect Monday to Friday until 9pm and Saturday and Sunday until 6pm. If there are no parking meters in sight, look for computerized Pay 'N Go stations, which are rapidly replacing meters. They're black metal kiosks about 1.8m (6 ft.) tall with a white "P" in a blue circle. Press the "English" button, enter the letter from the space where you are parked, then pay with cash or a credit card, following the on-screen instructions.

Most downtown shopping complexes have underground parking lots, as do the big downtown hotels. Some of the hotels allow guests "in/out privileges" for free, which can save money if you plan to do some sightseeing by car.

2

Fast **Facts**

AREA CODES Montréal area codes are **514** and **438.** Outside of Montréal, the area code for the southern Laurentides is **450** and the northern Laurentides, from Val David up, uses **819**. The Cantons-de-l'Est are the same: **450** or **819**, depending on how close you are to Montréal. Starting in October 2010, new telephone numbers in the 450 region may be given the area code **438.** You always need to dial the three-digit area code in addition to the seven-digit number. Numbers that begin with **800, 888, 877,** or **866** are free to call from Canada and the U.S.

ATMS/CASHPOINTS Automated teller machines are as ubiquitous in the Québec province and the rest of Canada as they are in the U.S. and Europe. In French they're called GABs, or *guichet automatique bancaire.* They're sometimes referred to as "cash machines" or "cashpoints." ATMs are found outside or inside bank branches, in malls, at train stations, and in small shops. They're as common in small villages as they are in the cities. Look for signs reading GUICHET AUTOMATIQUE or SERVICES AUTOMATISES.

Note about PINs: PINs (personal identification numbers) can only be four digits at Canadian ATMs. If your PIN has more numbers, change it before departing—otherwise your card will not work. Be sure you also know your daily withdrawal limit before you depart.

AUTOMOBILE ORGANIZATIONS Members of the American Automobile Association (AAA) are covered by the Canadian Automobile Association (CAA) while traveling in Canada. Bring your membership card and proof of insurance. The 24-hour hot line for emergency road service is ☎ **800/222-4357.** The AAA card will also provide discounts at a wide variety of hotels and restaurants in Québec province. Visit www.caa quebec.com for more information.

BABYSITTERS Many Montréal hotels offer some form of babysitting service. If not, your hotel's concierge should be able to help you find a reliable babysitter.

B&BS The **Association des Gites Touristiques de Montréal** (the Bed & Breakfast Association of Montréal; 1933 rue Panet; ☎ **514/510-7976;** www.agtm.ca) lists B&Bs and guesthouses that are approved by the province's tourist board. You can also find B&Bs at www.tourisme-montreal.org.

BANKS Banks are generally open from 8 or 9am to 4pm Monday to Friday. Most major Canadian banks have branches on either rue Sherbrooke or rue Ste-Catherine.

BIKE RENTALS In 2009, the city initiated a long-awaited self-service bicycle rental program called **BIXI** (www.bixi.com), a combination of the words *bicyclette* and *taxi.* It's similar to programs in Paris and Berlin, where users pick up BIXI bikes from designated stands throughout the city and drop them off at any other stand, for a small fee. Some 3,000 bikes were to be in operation by the end of 2009 with some 300 stations in Montréal's central boroughs. For short trips (under 2 hr.), it's economical, but if you want a bike for a half-day or longer, it's probably cheaper to rent from a shop such as **ÇaRoule/Montréal on Wheels** (27 rue de la Commune est; ☎ **877/866-0633** or 514/866-0633; www.caroulemontreal.com), on the waterfront road bordering Vieux-Port.

BUSINESS HOURS Most stores in the province are open from 9 or 10am until 6pm Monday through Wednesday, 9am to 9pm on Thursday and Friday, 9am to 5pm on Saturday, and from noon to 5pm on Sunday. Since November 2008, stores in downtown Montréal have been able to stay open until 8pm on Saturday and Sunday, an 18-month change in law that's part of a government-sanctioned pilot project to stimulate tourism.

CONSULATES & EMBASSIES Embassies are located in Ottawa, Canada's capital, but there are consulate offices throughout the Canadian provinces. The **U.S. Embassy** information line is ☎ **888/840-0032** and costs C$1.59 per minute. The U.S. has a consulate in Montréal at 1155 rue St-Alexandre (☎ **514/398-9695**) where nonemergency American citizen services are provided, by appointment only. The **U.K.'s consulate** in Montréal is at 1000 rue de la Gauchetière ouest, Ste. 4200 (☎ **514/866-5863**). For contact information for other embassies and consulates, search for "Foreign Representatives in Canada" at www.international.gc.ca.

CURRENCY EXCHANGE Avoid exchanging money at commercial exchange bureaus and hotels, which often have the highest transaction fees. The best rates will come from withdrawing money upon arrival at an ATM. That said, you can exchange currency at train stations, hotels, and exchange booths all over the city. Some Montréal establishments will accept U.S. currency.

CUSTOMS Bringing normal baggage and personal possessions into Canada should be no problem, but plants, animals, and other products may be prohibited or require additional documents before they're allowed in. Tobacco and alcoholic beverages face strict import restrictions: Individuals 18 years or older are allowed to bring in, for free, 200 cigarettes, 50 cigars, or 200 grams of tobacco; and 1.14 liters of liquor, 1.5 liters of wine, or 24 cans or bottles of beer. Additional amounts face hefty taxes. For specific information about Canadian rules, check with the **Canada Border Services Agency** online at www.cbsa-asfc.gc.ca. Search for "bsf5082" for a full list of visitor information.

DINING Restaurants are colloquially called "restos" in the Québec province. Many moderately priced bistros offer outstanding food, congenial surroundings, and amiable service at reasonable prices. Nearly all have menus posted outside, making it easy to do a little comparison shopping. While many restaurants are open all day between meals, some shut down between lunch and dinner. Most restaurants serve until 9:30pm or 10pm.

To dine for less, have your main meal at lunch or veer toward *table d'hôte* **(fixed-price) meals.** An entire two- to four-course meal, often with a beverage, can be had for little more than the price of an a la carte main course alone.

It's wise to make a reservation if you wish to dine at one of the city's top restaurants, especially on a Friday or Saturday evening. Unlike in larger American and European cities, a day or two in advance is sufficient for most places on most days. A hotel concierge can make the reservation, though nearly all restaurant hosts will switch immediately to English when they sense that a caller doesn't speak French. Except in a handful of luxury restaurants, there are no dress codes. But

Montréalers are a fashionable lot and manage to look smart even in casual clothes. Adults who show up in T-shirts and jeans may feel uncomfortably out of place at most Montréal establishments.

DOCTORS See "Hospitals," below.

DRINKING LAWS The legal drinking age in the province is 18. All hard liquor and spirits in Québec are sold through official government stores operated by the Québec Société des Alcools (look for maroon signs with the acronym SAQ). Wine and beer are available in grocery stores and convenience stores, called *dépanneurs*. Bars can pour drinks as late as 3am, but often stay open later.

Penalties for drunk driving in Canada are heavy. Provisions instituted in 2008 include higher mandatory penalties including a minimum fine of C$1,000 for a first offense, and for a second offense, a minimum of 30 days in jail. Drivers caught under the influence face a maximum life sentence if they cause death, and a maximum 10-year sentence if they cause bodily harm.

DRUGSTORES A pharmacy is called a *pharmacie;* a drugstore is a *droguerie.* A large chain in Montréal is **Pharmaprix.** Its branch at 5122 Côte-des-Neiges (☎ **514/738-8464;** www.pharmaprix.ca) is open 24 hours a day, 7 days a week, and has a fairly convenient location.

ELECTRICITY Like the U.S., Canada uses 110 to 120 volts AC (60 cycles), compared to the 220 to 240 volts AC (50 cycles) used in most of Europe, Australia, and New Zealand. If your small appliances use 220 to 240 volts, you'll need a 110-volt transformer and a plug adapter with two flat parallel pins to operate them in Canada. They can be difficult to find in Canada, so bring one with you.

EMERGENCIES Dial ☎ **911** for police, firefighters, or an ambulance.

EVENT LISTINGS For listings of performances or special events, pick up a free copy of *Montréal Scope* (www.montrealscope.com), a monthly ads-and-events booklet usually available in hotel lobbies, or the free weekly papers *Mirror* (www.montrealmirror.com) and *Hour* (www.hour.ca), both in English. *Fugues* (www.fugues.com) provides news and views of gay and lesbian events, clubs, restaurants, and activities. One fun blog about city happenings is **Midnight Poutine** (www.midnightpoutine.ca), a self-described "delicious high-fat source of rants, raves and musings." Also see "Newspapers & Magazines," below.

FAMILY TRAVEL Montréal offers an abundance of family-oriented activities. Many of them are outdoors, even in winter. Watersports, river cruises, fort climbing, and fireworks displays are among summer's many attractions, with dog sledding and skiing the top choices in snowy months. For accommodations, restaurants, and attractions that are particularly kid friendly, look for the "Kids" icon throughout this guide. Also see "Montréal with Kids" on p 56. For a list of more family-friendly travel resources, visit www.frommers.com/planning.

GASOLINE (PETROL) Gasoline in Canada is more expensive than in the U.S., even considering the steep rise in U.S. costs over the past few years. Europeans will find the prices inexpensive. Gas is sold by the liter, and 3.78 liters equals 1 gallon. Recent prices of C$.93 per liter are the equivalent of about US$2.85 per gallon.

GAY & LESBIAN TRAVELERS Montréal has one of the largest and most visible gay communities in North

America. Gay life here is generally open and accepted (gay marriage is legal in the Québec province), and gay and lesbian travelers are heavily marketed to. Tourisme Montréal has a "Gay and Lesbian" minisite (www.tourisme-montreal.org/Traveller/Gay-and-Lesbian) which lists gay-friendly accommodations, events, websites for queer meet ups, and more. Many travelers head straight to the Village (also known as "the Gay Village"), a neighborhood located primarily along rue Ste-Catherine est between rue St-Hubert and rue Papineau where there are antiques shops, bars, B&Bs, and clubs, clubs, clubs. The Beaudry Métro station is at the heart of the neighborhood and marked by a rainbow flag. (As the Tourisme Montréal website says, "Rainbow columns on a subway station entrance? I've got a feeling we're not in Kansas anymore!") The **Village Tourism Information Centre** (249, rue Saint-Jacques, Ste. 302; ☎ 888/595-8110 or 514/522-1885), is open Tuesday through Thursday in the summer and Monday through Friday the rest of the year, and provides information about everything from wine bars to yoga classes.

HOLIDAYS   Canada's important public holidays are New Year's Day (Jan 1); Good Friday and Easter Monday (Mar or Apr); Victoria Day (the Mon preceding May 25); St-Jean-Baptiste Day, Québec's "national" day (June 24); Canada Day (July 1); Labour Day (first Mon in Sept); Canadian Thanksgiving Day (second Mon in Oct); and Christmas (Dec 25).

HOSPITALS   Hospitals with emergency rooms include **Hôpital Général de Montréal** (1650 rue Cedar; ☎ 514/934-1934) and **Hôpital Royal Victoria** (687 av. des Pins ouest; ☎ 514/934-1934). **Hôpital de Montréal pour Enfants** (2300 rue Tupper; ☎ 514/412-4400), is a children's hospital. All three are associated with McGill University.

INSURANCE   **Medical Insurance** Medical treatment in Canada isn't free for foreigners, and hospitals make you pay your bills at the time of service. Check whether your insurance policy covers you while traveling in Canada, especially for hospitalization abroad. U.S. Medicare and Medicaid programs do not provide coverage for hospital or medical costs outside the U.S. Many other policies require you to pay for services upfront and, if they reimburse you at all, will only do so after you return home. Carry details of your insurance plan with you, and leave a copy with a friend at home. U.K. nationals also have to pay for medical treatment in Canada.

Travel Insurance   The cost of travel insurance varies widely, depending on the destination, the cost and length of your trip, your age and health, and the type of trip you're taking, but expect to pay between 4% and 8% of the cost of the vacation. You can get estimates from various providers at www.insuremytrip.com. Enter your trip cost and dates, your age, and other information for prices from more than a dozen companies. U.K. citizens and their families who make more than one trip abroad per year may find that an annual travel insurance policy works out to be a better deal. Check www.money supermarket.com, which compares prices across a wide range of providers for single- and multitrip policies.

Trip-Cancellation Insurance Trip-cancellation insurance will help retrieve your money if you have to back out of a trip or depart early, or if your travel supplier goes bankrupt. Trip cancellation usually covers such events as sickness and natural disasters. The latest news in trip-cancellation insurance is the availability of any-reason cancellation coverage, which costs more but covers cancellations made for any reason. You won't get back 100% of your trip's cost, but you'll be refunded a substantial portion. **TravelSafe** (☎ 888/885-7233; www.travelsafe.com) offers both types of coverage. Expedia also offers any-reason cancellation coverage for its air-hotel packages. For details, contact one of the following recommended insurers: **Access America** (☎ 800/284-8300; www.accessamerica.com), **Travel Guard International** (☎ 800/826-4919; www.travelguard.com), **Travel Insured International** (☎ 800/243-3174; www.travelinsured.com), or **Travelex Insurance Services** (☎ 800/228-9792; www.travelex-insurance.com).

For more information on medical insurance while traveling, travel insurance, and trip-cancellation insurance, please visit www.frommers.com/planning.

INTERNET ACCESS Nearly all hotels and most *auberges* and cafes now offer Wi-Fi. Many hotels also still offer high-speed Internet access through cable connections. Most large hotels maintain business centers with computers for use by guests or outsiders, and most of the smaller boutique hotels now have at least one computer available for guests. Cybercafes are fading from the Canadian scene with the rise of Wi-Fi, but there are still a few around. In Vieux-Montréal, **Café-Bistro Van Houtte** (165 rue St-Paul ouest; ☎ **514/288-9387**), has a bank of computers and prepaid Internet access cards for C$5.65 per hour.

LANGUAGE Canada is officially bilingual, but the Québec province has laws that make French mandatory in signage. About 80% of Montréal's population speaks French as a first language. Still, an estimated four out of five Francophones (French speakers) speak at least some English. Hotel desk staff, sales clerks, and telephone operators nearly always greet people initially in French, but usually switch to English quickly if necessary. Outside of Montréal, visitors are more likely to encounter residents who don't speak English. If smiles and sign language don't work, look around for a young person—most of them study English in school.

LAUNDROMATS Laundromats aren't thick upon the ground in tourist districts. In Montréal, one option is **Buanderie Chez Bobette** (850 rue Duluth est; ☎ 514/522-2612), in the Plateau Mont-Royal neighborhood. **Kanji Laundry** offers free pickup and delivery within metro Montréal (☎ 514/501-3577; http://kanji laundry.com) and can launder or dry clean within 24 hours.

LEGAL AID If you are arrested, your country's embassy or consulate can provide the names of attorneys who speak English. See "Consulates & Embassies," above.

LOST PROPERTY Keep a list of both credit card numbers and the emergency telephone numbers on the back of each in a separate place. (One easy method is to make photo copies of all their fronts and backs.) That way, if you discover your wallet has been lost or stolen, you can easily notify all of your credit card companies. Also file a report at the nearest police precinct; your credit card company or insurer may require a police report to process a claim. If you lose something on the Métro, call ☎ 514/786-4636 and follow the prompts to report your missing belongings. Info is online at www. stm.info/English/info/a-objets.htm.

MAIL & POSTAGE All mail sent through **Canada Post** (☎ **866/607-6301** or 416/979-8822; www. canadapost.ca) must bear Canadian stamps. A letter or postcard to the U.S. requires C\$.98. A letter or postcard to anywhere else costs C\$1.65. To mail within Canada, letters cost C\$.54. **FedEx** (☎ **800/463-3339;** www.fedex.com/ca) also offers service from Canada.

Money Canadian money comes in graduated denominations of dollars and cents. New bills featuring tougher security measures, bolder colors, and more modern designs are being introduced into circulation. Bills start at C\$5 and go up. Coins include one-dollar and two-dollar denominations, nicknamed the Loonie (for a one-dollar coin) and the Toonie (for a two-dollar coin).

At press time, the Canadian dollar was worth US81¢, 56p, and .62€. Credit or debit cards are accepted at almost all shops, restaurants, and hotels, but you should always keep some cash on hand for small venues that don't take plastic.

NEWSPAPERS & MAGAZINES Montréal's primary English-language newspaper is the **Montréal Gazette** (www.montrealgazette. com). For information about current arts happenings in Montréal, pick up the Friday or Saturday edition of the Gazette. The **Globe and Mail** (www.theglobeandmail.com) is a national English-language paper. Most large newsstands and those in larger hotels carry the New York Times, Wall Street Journal, and International Herald Tribune.

PARKING See "By Car" in the "Getting Around" section, earlier in this chapter.

PASSES The **Montréal Museums Pass** is an excellent option for ambitious sightseers. It allows entry to 34 of the city's museums and attractions and is good for 3 consecutive days. The full price, C\$50, includes unlimited access to public transportation along with the museums. A card for just the museums costs C\$45. There are no separate rates for seniors or children. The pass is available at all participating museums, many hotels, and the tourist offices at 174 rue Notre-Dame (in Vieux-Montréal) and 1255 rue Peel (downtown). Find out more at www. montrealmuseums.org.

PASSPORTS Passport rules for travelers from the U.S. to Canada are now similar to rules for all other international travelers to the country: A passport, passport card, or Western Hemisphere Travel Initiative document is required for entry. For U.S. citizens, the passport requirement has been changing over the past few years as part of the U.S. Intelligence Reform and Terrorism Prevention Act of 2004. Since January 2007, all air travelers have been required to present a valid passport, and as of June 1, 2009, the same requirements apply to everyone 16 years old and up traveling by land or sea, including trips by car, bus, or cruise ship. U.S. citizens under 16 will be able to continue using a U.S. birth certificate or naturalization certificate (original only, not a photocopy) at land and sea borders. Details are online at http://travel. state.gov.

Make a copy of your passport's information page and keep it separate from your passport in case of loss or theft. For emergency passport replacement, contact your country's embassy or consulate (see "Consulates & Embassies," earlier in this chapter).

POLICE Dial ☎ **911** for police, fire-fighters, or an ambulance. Most local police speak both French and English, and members of the RCMP (Royal Canadian Mounted Police) are required to be bilingual.

SAFETY Montréal is an extremely safe city, and far safer than its U.S. or European counterparts of similar size. Still, common sense insists that visitors stay alert and observe the usual urban precautions. It's best to stay out of parks at night and to take a taxi when returning from a late dinner or nightclub.

SENIOR TRAVELERS Throughout the Québec province, many theaters, museums, and other attractions offer reduced admission to people as young as 60. Many hotels also offer senior discounts. If you have an AAA card, show it: Members of the American Automobile Association get the same discounts as members of the CAA. That means reduced rates at a variety of museums, hotels, and restaurants.

SMOKING Smoking was banned in the province's bars, restaurants, clubs, casinos, and some other public spaces in 2006. Most small inns and many larger hotels have become entirely smoke free over the past few years as well.

SPECTATOR SPORTS Montréal hockey and football fans are a loyal bunch, so attending a home game can be quite an uplifting experience. The city's beloved NHL **Montréal Canadiens** (☎ **877/668-8269** or 514/790-2525; www.canadiens. com) have won the Stanley Cup over 20 times, and devoted fans pack the Centre Bell to cheer on Les Habitants. Fans of U.S.-style football pack McGill University's Percival-Molson Memorial Stadium to cheer on the **Montréal Alouettes**

(☎ 514/871-2255; www.montreal alouettes.com), the city's professional team.

TAXES Most goods and services in Canada are taxed 5% by the federal government (the GST, or Goods and Services Tax). On top of that, the province of Québec tacks on an additional 7.5% tax (the TVQ). A 3% accommodations tax is in effect in Montréal. Nonresident visitors used to be able to apply for a tax rebate, but that practice was eliminated in 2007.

TAXIS See "By Taxi" in the "Getting Around" section, earlier in this chapter.

TELEPHONES The Canadian telephone system, operated by Bell Canada, closely resembles the U.S. model. All operators speak English and French, and respond in the appropriate language as soon as callers speak to them. In Canada, dial ☎ **00** to reach an operator.

When making a local call within Québec province, you must dial the area code before the seven-digit number.

Phone numbers that begin with 800, 888, 877, and 866 are toll free. That means they're free to call within Canada and from the U.S. You need to dial 1 first. A local call at a pay phone in the Québec province costs C$.50. Directory information calls (dial ☎ 411) are free of charge. Remember that in hotels, both local as well as long-distance calls usually cost more—sometimes a lot more. Some hotels charge you for *all* phone calls you make, including toll-free ones.

TICKETS Call venues individually for specific ticket information. Tickets at large stadiums are often handled by outside ticket companies and have large fees associated with them. For last-minute as well as future-event tickets, visit **Vitrine Culturelle de Montréal** (145 rue Ste-Catherine ouest; ☎ 866/924-5538 or 514/285-4545; www.vitrineculturelle.com), a discount ticket office for cultural events. It's in front of the Place des Arts.

TIPPING In restaurants, bars, and nightclubs, tip waiters 15% to 20% of the check, tip checkroom attendants C$1 per garment, and tip valet-parking attendants C$1 per vehicle. In hotels, tip bellhops C$1 per bag and tip the chamber staff C$3 to C$5 per day. Tip taxi drivers 15% of the fare; tip skycaps at airports C$1 per bag; and tip hairdressers and barbers 15% to 20%.

TOILETS You won't find public toilets on the streets in Montréal or Québec City, but they can be found in tourist offices, museums, railway and bus stations, service stations, and large shopping complexes. Restaurants and bars in heavily visited areas often reserve their restrooms for patrons.

TOURIST OFFICES The main tourist office is the **Infotouriste Centre** (1255 rue Peel; ☎ 877/266-5687 or 514/873-2015; Métro: Peel). It's open daily and the bilingual staff can provide suggestions for accommodations, dining, car rentals, and attractions. In Vieux-Montréal, there's a small tourist information office at 174 rue Notre-Dame est, at the corner of Place Jacques-Cartier (Métro: Champ-de-Mars). It's open daily in warmer months, Wednesday through Sunday in winter.

TOURS An introductory guided tour is often the best and most efficient way to begin exploring a new city, and can give you a good lay of the land and overview of Montréal's history. **Gray Line de Montréal** (☎ 514/934-1222; www.coach canada.com) offers commercial guided tours in air-conditioned buses daily year-round. The basic city tour takes 3 hours and costs C$40 for ages 12 and up, C$36 for seniors and students, C$28 for ages 5 to 11, and free for children 4 and younger. Tours depart from 1255 rue Peel. **Amphi-Bus** (☎ 514/849-5181; www.montreal-amphibus-tour.com) is something a little different: It tours Vieux-Montréal much like any other bus until it waddles into the waters of the harbor for a dramatic finish. Departures are on the hour from 10am until midnight June through September, and at noon, 2, 4, and 6pm in May and October. Fares are C$32 for adults, C$29 for seniors, C$23 for students, C$18 for children 4 to 12, and C$10 for children 3 and younger. Reservations are required. The bus departs from the intersection of rue de la Commune and boulevard St-Laurent. **Le Bateau-Mouche** (☎ 800/361-9952 or 514/849-9952; www.bateau-mouche.com) is an air-conditioned, glass-enclosed vessel reminiscent of those on the Seine in Paris. It plies the St. Lawrence River from mid-May to mid-October, taking passengers on a route inaccessible by traditional vessels, passing under several bridges and providing sweeping views of the city, Mont-Royal, and the St. Lawrence and its islands. The 60-minute tours cost C$23 for adults, C$21 for seniors 65 and older and students, and C$11 for children 6 to 16, and are free for children 5 and younger. There also are 90-minute tours and dinner cruises.

For a complete listing of tours and tour operators, check under "Guided Tours" in the *Montréal Official Tourist Guide,* available at the downtown Infotouriste Centre (1255 rue Peel; ☎ 877/266-5687 or 514/873-2015; Métro: Peel).

TRAVELERS WITH DISABILITIES Québec regulations regarding wheelchair accessibility are similar to those in the U.S., including requirements for curb cuts, entrance ramps, designated parking spaces, and specially equipped bathrooms. However, access to the restaurants and inns housed in 18th- and 19th-century buildings, especially in Québec City, is often difficult or impossible. Advice for travelers with physical limitations is provided in the French-language guide *Le Québec Accessible* (2005), which lists more than 1,000 hotels, restaurants,

theaters, and museums. It costs C$20 and is available from **Kéroul** (☎ 514/252-3104; www.keroul. qc.ca). Kéroul also publishes an English-language brochure called *The Accessible Road,* which provides information about everything from how to get a handicapped parking sticker to which top attractions are most accessible. It's available as a free download at the Kéroul website. Also look for the **Tourist and Leisure Companion Sticker (T.L.C.S.)** at tourist sites; it designates that companions of travelers with disabilities can enter for free. A printable list of participating enterprises is online at www.vatl-tlcs.org.

Montréal: **A Brief History**

1535 A community of Iroquois establishes the village of Hochelaga in what's now called Montréal, living in 50 homes and farming the land. French explorer Jacques Cartier visits the village that year. When the French return in 1603, the village is empty. Other First Nations people, including the Algonquins and Hurons, also inhabit the region.

1608 Samuel de Champlain arrives in Québec City motivated by the burgeoning fur trade, obsessed with finding a route to China, and determined to settle "New France." Three years later, he establishes a fur trading post in Montréal where the Pointe-à-Callière now stands.

1617 Parisian apothecary Louis Hérbert and Mary Rollet become the first colonists in Québec City to live off the produce of their own farm.

1642 Ville-Marie is founded by Paul de Chomedy de Maisonneuve, who installs a wood cross at the top of Mont-Royal.

1670 Hudson Bay Company is incorporated by British royal charter, and the competition around the fur trade in the Québec province heightens tension between France and England.

1759 After over a century of conflict about who would rule the new world, the British defeat the French in Québec City and enter Montréal.

1760 Montréal falls to the British.

1763 The king of France cedes all of Canada to the king of England in the Treaty of Paris, ending the Seven Years' War.

1775 U.S. general George Washington and the U.S. Continental Congress decide to extend their rebellion north and take the

Québec province and the St. Lawrence River from the British, assuming that French-Canadians would happily join their cause. They predict wrongly. American Revolutionary forces occupy Montréal and Québec City after battles in 1775 and 1776 and then withdraw after a few months.

1821 English-speaking McGill University is established.

1824 The Lachine Canal opens after 3 years of construction, helping turn Montréal into a major port.

1833 Jacques Viger, born in Montréal in 1787, becomes the first mayor of Montréal.

1844 The Parliament of Canada is established in Montréal, though it later moves to Ottawa.

1852 The most devastating fire the city has experienced, known later as the Great Montréal Fire, leaves as many as 10,000 of the city's 57,000 inhabitants homeless and thousands without jobs in the middle of the hot, dry summer.

1857 The Gradual Civilization Act helps establish the Indian residential school system, a program of forced assimilation of First Nations children.

1859 Victoria Bridge is completed.

1924 A new, illuminated cross is unveiled on Mont-Royal on Christmas Day.

1933 Marché Atwater opens.

1939 The National Film Board is established.

1962 The city begins construction of the Métro system, which opens in 1966.

1962 With the construction of Place Ville-Marie, the Underground City is born.

1967 The Montréal World Exposition (Expo 67) is held and puts the city on glorious display to the world. The event is a major benchmark in the city's modern history.

1968 Parti Québécois is founded.

1968 Canadian soldiers take to the streets of Québec City to quell unrest by separatists.

1969 Montréal Expos, a Major League Baseball team, is established. The franchise later is relocated to Washington, D.C., in 2004, where it becomes the Washington Nationals.

1976 Montréal hosts the athletically successful but financially disastrous Summer Olympics, sending the city into years of monstrous debt.

1977 Bill 101 passes, all but banning the use of English on public signage in the Québec province.

1979 The Festival International de Jazz de Montréal is founded.

1985 Bill C-31 gives First Nations women the right to marry white men and keep their Indian status, a right long held by First Nations men.

1992 Montréal celebrates its 350th birthday.

1998 A January ice storm cripples the region, cutting off power to millions, causing massive damage to trees and property, and leaving a thick layer of ice across streets, buildings, and roofs.

1999 The definition of "spouse" is changed in 39 laws and regulations, eliminating all legal distinctions between same-sex and heterosexual couples and recognizing the legal status of same-sex civil unions.

2001 The federal and provincial government and the Cree Nation sign La Paix des Braves (The Peace of the Braves) allowing Hydro-Québec to set up hydroelectric plants on Cree land in exchange for C$3.5 billion.

2002 Construction of Palais des Congrès (Convention Center), an unlikely design triumph featuring transparent glass exterior walls in a crazy quilt of pink, yellow, blue, green, red, and purple rectangles, is completed.

2005 Gay marriage becomes legal in all Canadian provinces and territories.

2006 UNESCO, the United Nations Educational, Scientific and Cultural Organization, designates Montréal a UNESCO City of Design for "its ability to inspire synergy between public and private players" and reputation for design innovation.

2007 An anemic third-place showing by the Parti Québécois in provincial elections is read by many as a crushing defeat for both the party and the separatist movement.

2008 A report on provincial angst over so-called reasonable accommodation of minority religious practices declares, "Québec is at a turning point . . . The identity inherited from the French-Canadian past is perfectly legitimate and it must survive, but it can no longer occupy alone the Québec identity space."

The Politics of **Language & Identity**

Montréal and Québec City, the twin cities of the province of Québec, have a stronger European flavor than Canada's other municipalities. Most residents' first language is French, and a strong affiliation with France continues to be a central facet of the region's personality.

Many in Québec stayed committed to the French language and culture after British rule was imposed in 1759. Even with later waves of other immigrant populations pouring in over the cities, there was still a kind of bedrock loyalty held by many to the province's Gallic roots. Many Québécois continue to look across the Atlantic for inspiration in fashion, food, and the arts. Culturally and linguistically, it is that tenacious French connection that gives the province its special character.

In 1867, the British North America Act created the federation of the provinces of Québec, Ontario, Nova Scotia, and New Brunswick. It was a kind of independence for the region from Britain, but was unsettling for many French-Canadians, who wanted full autonomy. In 1883, Je me souviens—an ominous "I remember"—became the province's official motto.

In 1968, the Parti Québécois (PQ) was founded by René Lévesque, and the separatist movement began in earnest. One attempt to smooth ruffled Francophones (French speakers) was made in 1969, when federal legislation stipulated that all services across Canada were henceforth to be offered in both English and French, in effect declaring the nation bilingual.

That didn't assuage militant Québécois, however. They undertook to guarantee the primacy of French in their own province. To prevent dilution by newcomers, the children of immigrants were required to enroll in French-language schools, even if English or a third language was spoken in the home. This is still the case today. In 1977, Bill 101 passed, all but banning the use of English on public signage. The bill funded the establishment of enforcement units, a virtual language police who let no nit go unpicked. The resulting backlash provoked the flight of an estimated 400,000 Anglophones to other parts of Canada.

Support for the secessionist cause burgeoned again in Québec in the early 1990s, fueled by an election that firmly placed the PQ back in control of the provincial government. A referendum held in 1995 narrowly defeated succession from the Canadian union, but the vote settled nothing. The issue continued to divide families and dominate political discourse.

The year 2007 may have marked the beginning of the end the issue, however. In provincial elections, the Parti Québécois placed third with just 28% of the vote. The election was perceived by many as the first step in closing the door on the campaign for independence.

In the past 10 years, Montréal has become probably the most bilingual city in the world. Most people are comfortable speaking French, English, and a kind of Franglish patois that combines both.

Two other important cultural phenomena have emerged over the past 10 years. The first is an institutional acceptance of homosexuality. By changing the definition of "spouse" in 39 laws and regulations in 1999, Québec's government eliminated all legal distinctions between same-sex and heterosexual couples and became Canada's first province to recognize the legal status of same-sex civil unions. Gay marriage became legal in all of Canada's provinces and territories in 2005. Montréal, in particular, has transformed into one of North America's most welcoming cities for gay people.

The second phenomenon is an influx of even more immigrants into the province's melting pot. "Québec is at a turning point," declares a 2008 report about the province's angst over the so-called reasonable accommodation of minority religious practices, particularly those of Muslims and Orthodox Jews. "The identity inherited from the French-Canadian past is perfectly legitimate and it must survive," the report continues, "but it can no longer occupy alone the Québec identity space."

Together with 70,000 aboriginal people from 11 First Nations tribes who live in the province, immigrants help make the region as vibrant and alive as any on the continent.

Useful **Phrases & Menu Terms**

A word or two of halting French can go a long way in encouraging a French speaker to help you out. After all, you're asking your hosts to meet you much more than halfway in communicating. At the very least, practice basic greetings and the introductory phrase, Parlez-vous anglais? (Do you speak English?).

Useful Words & Phrases

ENGLISH	FRENCH	PRONUNCIATION
Yes/No	Oui/Non	wee/noh
Okay	D'accord	dah-core
Please	S'il vous plaît	seel voo play
Thank you	Merci	mair-see
You're welcome	De rien	duh ree-ehn
Hello (during daylight)	Bonjour	bohn-jhoor
Hello (at night)	Bonsoir	bohn-swahr
Goodbye	Au revoir	o vwahr
What's your name?	Comment vous appellez-vous?	kuh-mahn voo za-pell-ay-voo?
My name is	Je m'appelle	jhuh ma-pell
How are you?	Comment allez-vous?	kuh-mahn tahl-ay-voo?
So-so	Comme ci, comme ça	kum-see, kum-sah
I'm sorry/Excuse me	Pardon	pahr-dohn
Do you speak English?	Parlez-vous anglais?	par-lay-voo zahn-glay?
I don't speak French	Je ne parle pas français	jhuh ne parl pah frahn-say
I don't understand	Je ne comprends pas	jhuh ne kohm-prahn pas
Where is . . . ?	Où est . . . ?	ooh eh . . . ?
Why?	Pourquoi?	poor-kwah?
here/there	ici/là	ee-see/lah
left/right	à gauche/à droite	a goash/a drwaht
straight ahead	tout droit	too drwah
I want to get off at . . .	Je voudrais descendre à . . .	jhe voo-dray day-son-drah ah . . .
airport	l'aéroport	lair-o-por
bridge	pont	pohn
bus station	la gare d'autobus	lah gar duh aw-toh-boos
bus stop	l'arrêt de bus	lah-ray duh boohss
cathedral	cathedral	ka-tay-dral
church	église	ay-gleez
hospital	l'hôpital	low-pee-tahl
museum	le musée	luh mew-zay
police	la police	lah po-lees
one-way ticket	aller simple	ah-lay sam-pluh
round-trip ticket	aller-retour	ah-lay re-toor
ticket	un billet	uh bee-yay
toilets	les toilettes	lay twa-lets

In Your Hotel

ENGLISH	FRENCH	PRONUNCIATION
bathtub	une baignoire	ewn bayn-nwar
hot and cold water	l'eau chaude et froide	low showed ay fwad

ENGLISH	FRENCH	PRONUNCIATION
Is breakfast included?	Déjeuner inclus?	day-jheun-ay ehn-klu?
Room	une chambre	ewn shawm-bruh
shower	une douche	ewn dooch
sink	un lavabo	uh la-va-bow

The Calendar

ENGLISH	FRENCH	PRONUNCIATION
Sunday	dimanche	dee-mahnsh
Monday	lundi	luhn-dee
Tuesday	mardi	mahr-dee
Wednesday	mercredi	mair-kruh-dee
Thursday	jeudi	jheu-dee
Friday	vendredi	vawn-druh-dee
Saturday	samedi	sahm-dee
yesterday	hier	ee-air
today	aujourd'hui	o-jhord-dwee
this morning/this afternoon	ce matin/cet après-midi	suh ma-tan/set ah-preh mee-dee
tonight	ce soir	suh swahr
tomorrow	demain	de-man

Food, Menu & Cooking Terms

ENGLISH	FRENCH	PRONUNCIATION
I would like to eat	Je voudrais manger	jhe voo-dray mahn-jhay
Please give me	Donnez-moi, s'il vous plaît	doe-nay-mwah, seel voo play
a bottle of	une bouteille de	ewn boo-tay duh
a cup of	une tasse de	ewn tass duh
a glass of	un verre de	uh vair duh
a cocktail	un apéritif	uh ah-pay-ree-teef
the check/bill	l'addition/la note	la-dee-see-ohn/la noat
a knife	un couteau	uh koo-toe
a napkin	une serviette	ewn sair-vee-et
a spoon	une cuillère	ewn kwee-air
a fork	une fourchette	ewn four-shet
fixed-price menu	table d'hôte	tab-lah dote
Is the tip/service included?	Est-ce que le service est compris?	ess-ke luh ser-vees eh com-pree?
Waiter!/Waitress!	Monsieur!/Mademoiselle!	mun-syuh/mad-mwa-zel
wine list	une carte des vins	ewn cart day van
appetizer	une entrée	ewn en-tray
main course	un plat principal	uh plah pran-see-pahl
tip included	service compris	sehr-vees cohm-pree
tasting/chef's menu	menu dégustation	may-new day-gus-ta-see-on

Numbers

ENGLISH	FRENCH	PRONUNCIATION
0	zéro	zeh-roh
1	un	uhn
2	deux	duh
3	trois	twah
4	quatre	kah-truh
5	cinq	sank
6	six	seess
7	sept	set
8	huit	weet
9	neuf	nuhf
10	dix	deess
11	onze	ohnz
12	douze	dooz
13	treize	trehz
14	quatorze	kah-torz
15	quinze	kanz
16	seize	sez
17	dix-sept	deez-set
18	dix-huit	deez-weet
19	dix-neuf	deez-noof
20	vingt	vehn
30	trente	trahnt
40	quarante	kah-rahnt
50	cinquante	sang-kahnt
100	cent	sahn
1,000	mille	meel

Websites

Airlines

AIR CANADA
www.aircanada.ca
AIR FRANCE
www.airfrance.com
AMERICAN AIRLINES
www.aa.com
BRITISH AIRWAYS
www.british-airways.com
CONTINENTAL AIRLINES
www.continental.com
DELTA AIR LINES
www.delta.com
LUFTHANSA
www.lufthansa.com
OLYMPIC AIRLINES
www.olympicairlines.com

SWISS AIR
www.swiss.com
UNITED AIRLINES
www.united.com
US AIRWAYS
www.usairways.com

Car Rental Agencies

ADVANTAGE
www.advantage.com
ALAMO
www.alamo.com
AVIS
www.avis.com

BUDGET
www.budget.com
DOLLAR
www.dollar.com
ENTERPRISE
www.enterprise.com
HERTZ
www.hertz.com
NATIONAL
www.nationalcar.com
PAYLESS
www.paylesscarrental.com
THRIFTY
www.thrifty.com

Major Hotel & Motel Chains

BEST WESTERN INTERNATIONAL
www.bestwestern.com

CLARION HOTELS
www.choicehotels.com

COURTYARD BY MARRIOTT
www.marriott.com/courtyard

CROWNE PLAZA HOTELS
www.ichotelsgroup.com/crowneplaza

DAYS INN
www.daysinn.com

DOUBLETREE HOTELS
www.doubletree.com

ECONO LODGES
www.choicehotels.com

EMBASSY SUITES
www.embassysuites.com

FARFIELD INN BY MARRIOTT
www.farfieldinn.com

HAMPTON INN
http://hamptoninn1.hilton.com

HILTON HOTELS
www.hilton.com

HOLIDAY INN
www.holidayinn.com

HOWARD JOHNSON
www.hojo.com

HYATT
www.hyatt.com

INTERCONTINENTAL HOTELS & RESORTS
www.ichotelsgroup.com

LOEWS HOTELS
www.loewshotels.com

MARRIOTT
www.marriott.com

OMNI HOTELS
www.omnihotels.com

QUALITY
www.qualityinn.com

RADISSON HOTELS & RESORTS
www.radisson.com

RESIDENCE INN BY MARRIOTT
www.marriott.com/residenceinn

RODEWAY INNS
www.rodewayinn.com

SHERATON HOTELS & RESORTS
www.starwoodhotels.com/sheraton

SUPER 8 MOTELS
www.super8.com

TRAVELODGE
www.travelodge.com

WESTIN HOTELS & RESORTS
www.starwoodhotels.com/westin

WYNDHAM HOTELS & RESORTS
www.wyndham.com

Index

See also Accommodations and Restaurant indexes, below.

Photo **Credits**